"Duane Litfin's *Word versus Deed* addresses [...] for the church and pressing relevance for our own generation. Litfin is thoroughly convinced—on the basis of Scripture—that the gospel cannot be preached merely with deeds but must be proclaimed with words. He uses his extensive background in rhetoric and theology to explain why this is so and then employs his wisdom as a pastor to show the proper relationship between gospel words and gospel-worthy deeds in Christian life and witness."

Philip Ryken, President, Wheaton College

"Duane Litfin has written a book that needs to find its way into every preacher's briefcase or backpack—and quickly. With care and candor, he reminds us all of the Bible's priority of verbal proclamation. Evenhanded and deeply biblical, *Word versus Deed* does indeed reset the biblical balance. I am very thankful for this book, and you will be, too."

Al Mohler, President, The Southern Baptist Theological Seminary

"Today, as powerful voices inside and outside the church are insisting that the gospel is best proclaimed by deeds rather than words, Duane Litfin provides a wholly biblical answer that establishes the full primacy of proclamation together with the role of deeds in demonstrating the gospel to a watching world. Litfin's answer is finely wrought and judiciously reasoned as he travels the ladder of abstraction and the range of biblical revelation in respect to the preaching of the gospel. And it is utterly compelling. *Word versus Deed* is sure to be read, reread, and much discussed. This is a wise and timely book that brings biblical clarity to a life-and-death debate."

R. Kent Hughes, Senior Pastor Emeritus, College Church,
Wheaton, Illinois

"With interpretive skill and theological insight, Duane Litfin has given us a masterful treatment of the Bible's teaching regarding the necessity of gospel proclamation and the importance of good works. Litfin's thoughtful exegesis and pastoral wisdom provide helpful guidance that enables Christ followers to handle the difficult challenges associated with the themes of 'word' and 'deed' with greater responsibility. I am hopeful that this readable volume will point pastors, teachers, and church leaders toward a more informed understanding of God's Word—resulting in faithful living *and* convictional proclamation."

David S. Dockery, President, Union University

"Many people like to make us pick between word and deed as the best way to reflect our Christian call. It is choice we need not make. In a book that shows how both word and deed are important and necessary, Duane Litfin also reminds us how important having the Word is. It is a needed reminder that allows us to reflect on how to live our Christian lives in balance, both proclaiming and reflecting the truth that God is at work among us."

Darrell L. Bock, Research Professor of New Testament Studies,
Dallas Theological Seminary; author of over 30 books

"Getting the pendulum of truth to cease its drift from side to side is a perpetual challenge. For many decades in the not-too-distant past, the gospel was a proclamational priority with little emphasis on the gospel's call to feed the hungry, care for the poor, and break the bonds of oppression. The social gospel was what those 'liberals' did. Many of us have now lived long enough to watch the pendulum swing to the opposite extreme with the deeds of the gospel being seemingly sufficient. Thankfully, my friend Duane Litfin has articulately and persuasively brought these issues of the gospel into balance. His fresh, intriguing treatment of key passages and his usual precision in developing an argument make a much needed contribution that leads us to empower the gospel with both word and deed."

    Joseph M. Stowell, President, Cornerstone University

"There must be a sharp distinction between the gospel—the message about what God has done in Jesus, supremely in his death and resurrection—and how the Christian acts as an implication of the gospel. This book is a positive, helpful articulation of the importance of maintaining the distinction between the gospel preached (word) and the gospel lived (deed)."

    Ben Peays, Executive Director, The Gospel Coalition

To Peter & Mary Blessings.
Alozemba & Mercy Unoiegbu.

Congratulations, young man

Love & Patti King

Walter & Ediel Wiens

WORD
vs
DEED

WORD
DEED

WORD VERSUS DEED

RESETTING THE SCALES TO A BIBLICAL BALANCE

DUANE LITFIN

CROSSWAY

WHEATON, ILLINOIS

Cover design: Jon McGrath, Simplicated Studio

First printing 2012

Printed in the United States of America

Unless otherwise indicated, Scripture quotations are from the ESV® Bible (*The Holy Bible, English Standard Version*®), copyright © 2001 by Crossway. Used by permission. All rights reserved.

Scripture references marked NIV are taken from *The Holy Bible, New International Version*®, NIV®. Copyright © 1973, 1978, 1984, 2011 by Biblica, Inc.™ Used by permission. All rights reserved worldwide.

Scripture references marked NKJV are from *The New King James Version*. Copyright © 1982, Thomas Nelson, Inc. Used by permission.

All emphases in Scripture quotations have been added by the author.

Trade paperback ISBN: 978-1-4335-3112-5

PDF ISBN: 978-1-4335-3113-2

Mobipocket ISBN: 978-1-4335-3114-9

ePub ISBN: 978-1-4335-3115-6

Library of Congress Cataloging-in-Publication Data

Litfin, A. Duane.
   Word versus deed : resetting the scales to a biblical balance / Duane Litfin.
      p. cm.
   Includes bibliographical references.
   ISBN 978-1-4335-3112-5 (tp)
   1. Communication—Religious aspects—Christianity. 2. Christian life. I. Title.
BV4597.53.C64L58   2012
248.4—dc23   2011051831

To all those faithful disciples at Wheaton College—students,
staff, faculty, board, alumni—who have encouraged
and instructed me by their balanced commitment
to both word and deed in serving Jesus Christ.

Whatever you do, in word or deed, do everything
in the name of the Lord Jesus, giving thanks
to God the Father through him.

—Colossians 3:17

CONTENTS

INTRODUCTION

WORDS OR DEEDS?

Preach the gospel at all times.
Use words if necessary.

—Anonymous

The goal of this book is simple enough: to offer thoughtful Christians some help in thinking biblically about the enduring question of *word* versus *deed* in their Christian calling.[1]

The issue here, of course, is one of balance. How are Christians to think about the relative roles of *word* and *deed* in what Christ has called his people to be and do? The church has often gotten this balance wrong over the centuries, and if much of the current dialog on the subject is any measure, our own generation may be following suit. This book is about seeking a proper *biblical* balance between these two dimensions of the Christian's calling, which is to say, it's about setting the scales to a balance that is true to the Scriptures.

This sounds simple. But finding and maintaining a biblical balance on such a complex subject is anything but easy. It's like walking a tightrope. There is only one path that will keep us upright and moving forward, but there are many ways to fall to one side or the other.

Misguided claims in the historic "word versus deed" debate abound. On the surface some of them sound plausible, and all the more so as they are often-repeated. But left unchallenged these mistaken notions, like winds aloft, jostle and buffet us, making it difficult to keep our thinking and behavior balanced. Only by measuring these notions against the Scriptures can we resist their buffeting and maintain the equilibrium the Lord intends for his church.

MISGUIDED NOTIONS

What sort of misguided notions do we have in mind? Here's a prominent example.

It would be hard to overstate how often we hear these days, expressed with passion and hearty approval, the famous dictum attributed to Francis of Assisi: "Preach the gospel at all times. Use words if necessary." In this saying, the "word versus deed" question rears its head, stressing in this instance how important it is for Christians to "preach the gospel" with their actions. According to this way of thinking, deeds may trump words when it comes to communicating the gospel. Let the gospel be seen rather than spoken, it is said. Words may serve a useful backup role, to be used as needed, but our actions must take center stage if we are to make a difference in the world.

At first blush this sounds right. Except that it isn't.

First, according to those who know about such things, St. Francis never uttered this saying. The Franciscans are a religious order founded by St. Francis. They are experts on his life and teaching, and it is they who insist that, after diligent research, they can find no record of St. Francis ever expressing this maxim. It appears nowhere in his writings or even in his early biographies. No one can find any record of this saying within two centuries of Francis's death.[2]

More importantly, however, if we accept this dictum at face value, we open ourselves to confusion. It's simply not possible to preach the gospel without words. The gospel is inherently a *verbal* thing, and preaching the gospel is inherently a *verbal* behavior. Thus the implication of this saying—that we are daily "preaching the gospel" with our deeds—is seriously misguided. It's a mistake which, as we shall see, can lead to a range of unfortunate results.

A LIGHTER TOUCH

But perhaps we should lighten up, we may say. Let's treat this saying a bit more delicately. Let us view it merely as an *aphorism* and avoid pressing its language too literally. According to this reading, the saying is merely a rhetorical trope designed to emphasize the importance of backing up our gospel words with Christ-following lives.

This, of course, is an immensely important and thoroughly biblical idea. If this is all our maxim is affirming we should deem it very useful indeed. But, unfortunately, this is not all it's affirming. Many seem to want to treat it much more literally, precisely because they see no difficulty in doing so. They will insist that the gospel can indeed be preached without words. Sometimes this is referred to as an "incarnational" approach to evangelism, whereby we "preach the gospel" by incarnating it in the world. You can preach the gospel with words, it is said, and you can preach the gospel with your actions. In fact, between the two our actions may be the more important because they speak louder than our words. Some even assert that without the actions to back them up, the words can have little impact.

What should we make of this claim? Can we or can we not "preach the gospel" with our actions? Who's right, and does it really matter?

As it happens, it matters a great deal. The stakes are surprisingly high in how we decide this question. So we need to be careful to test our answer against the Scriptures.

IMPORTANT QUESTIONS

If you believe the gospel can be preached without words, this book is for you. I hope to challenge your thinking and lay out a more fully biblical way of thinking about the issue. On the other hand, if you believe the gospel cannot be preached without words, this book is also for you. My goal is to support you in that conviction and explore with you the implications of your claim.

This effort will take us into some interesting and important territory. What after all is the gospel, and what is evangelism? What is the role of our deeds in fulfilling Christ's calling? How is Scripture being used and misused in this discussion, and how do these mistakes wind up distorting our understanding of the relevant issues, not to mention our behavior? These are the sorts of questions this book attempts to address.

As I have said, the stakes in this discussion are higher than one might guess. This is not some esoteric debate reserved for theologians or technical Bible scholars. Faithful obedience to Jesus Christ is what we're after, and that applies to all who call him Lord. Such obedience must by definition begin with clear thinking about what Jesus is calling us to be and do, for if we do not understand our calling, what are the chances we will fulfill it? This is what's on the line in our discussion.

THINKING BIBLICALLY

Our goal in this book is to think biblically about the issues of "word versus deed" in the Christian's calling. But even as I write this sentence I'm aware that not all will consider this a worthy or even achievable goal.

First, there are those who, to put it mildly, demonstrate little confidence in the Scriptures. In his *Letters from the Earth,* Mark Twain said of the Bible, "It is full of interest. It has noble poetry in it; and some clever fables; and some blood-drenched history; and some good morals; and a wealth of obscenity; and upwards of a thousand lies." From today's popular atheists one can hear similar sentiments. We would not expect such critics to be much interested in thinking *biblically*.

There are others who will cite the Bible when it says something of which they approve but who are also not the least inclined to treat it as an authoritative word from God. They quote the Bible the way we might quote Shakespeare, because they find something there particularly apt and well put. But they do not come to the Scriptures for divine direction.

Then there are those who view the Bible as a loose collection of religious writings produced by scores of authors and editors over hundreds of years. As such, the biblical writings lack coherence. Hence the notion of something being "biblical," in any sense that requires a Bible that speaks with a unified voice, is misguided. The Bible manifests no such unified voice, they will argue. It speaks with many voices and says a variety of different, often contradictory things. There is therefore no such thing as a coherent "biblical" viewpoint to discover.

Still others wish to view the Scriptures in a more positive light, but they nonetheless do not look to the Bible for the sort of direction we have in mind in this book—or, at least, they are disinclined to discover that direction by searching out the details of the biblical text. Their strategy is less exegetical than theological, or even philosophical. They prefer to extrapolate the Bible's relevance from its grand, mountaintop themes: creation, fall, redemption, and consummation. Exploring the full range of what the Bible actually says about a question such as ours appears to hold little interest for these thinkers. They may even dismiss such efforts as an exercise in proof-texting.

OUR WORKING ASSUMPTION TAKE NOTE!

So let it be said at the outset that our working assumption in this book is the historic claim that the Bible, in its entirety, is

God's inscripturated Word. It is therefore unified, consistent, and authoritative. Through all its manifest variety of voices, topics, and types of literature, it evinces an underlying coherence attributable to its ultimate source—it is *God's* Word. Its writings (the *graphe*) were "outbreathed" by God and are therefore profitable "for teaching, rebuking, correcting and training in righteousness," with a view to equipping us thoroughly "for every good work" (2 Tim. 3:16–17 NIV). With generations of Christians who have gone before, we therefore look to the Bible as our "only rule of faith and practice." It speaks to us reliably not only of the grand mountaintop themes of the Christian *faith*—a point on which I not only concur but will insist—but also of more specific issues of our Christian *practice*. It thus provides us "the whole counsel of God" (Acts 20:27), including counsel toward a balanced understanding of the church's calling.

> Scripture is the fundamental source for one's speaking with a Christian voice and acting out of Christian conviction.
> —Nicholas Wolterstroff

With this assumption in place, we want to inquire about what the Bible has to say on the important subject of word versus deed. We will explore the full range of this biblical counsel, yet we will also work to avoid the pitfalls of claiming the Bible's authority for what it does not, in fact, teach. Faithful students of Scripture must do no less.

HANDLING THE TEXT

It is not uncommon, unfortunately, to find the Bible handled rather loosely in the "word versus deed" discussion, even by those who consider themselves its friends. Wishing to enlist its authority for their cause, they seem unconcerned about bending its unwary texts to their own purposes.

Such cavalier treatments of Scripture are puzzling. If we

do not consider the Bible to be normative and authoritative, why cite it at all? Leave it out of the discussion. But if we do consider it to be God's authoritative Word, it would seem we should place the highest premium on handling its texts with integrity, making every effort, to the best of our ability as fallible interpreters, to understand and represent them aright. The alternative, we were long ago warned, bears serious consequences:

> Let the prophet who has a dream tell the dream, but let him who has my word speak my word faithfully. What has straw in common with wheat? declares the LORD. Is not my word like fire, declares the LORD, and like a hammer that breaks the rock in pieces? Therefore, behold, I am against the prophets, declares the LORD, who steal my words from one another. Behold, I am against the prophets, declares the LORD, who use their tongues and declare, declares the LORD. (Jer. 23:28–31)

In this book we draw upon the entire Bible—Law, Prophets, Wisdom, Gospels (both the Synoptics and John), Epistles (both Pauline and general), even apocalyptic. We will range widely throughout the Scriptures, assuming we will find there a complex and multidimensional but also coherent and, in the end, unified witness on our important topic. This also means, of course, that we will incur a special obligation to avoid "proof-texting" in our discussion; that is, we must avoid decontextualizing passages of the Bible in such a way as to distort or misrepresent their meaning.

Context is always a critical issue in the study of Scripture. Any fair use of a passage of the Bible must give due consideration to the natural habitat from which it is drawn. Without that, the biblical text can easily be put to purposes its divine and human authors never envisioned. This, in turn, is a surefire way to lose the balance between word and deed that Christ desires for his church. In the latter chapters of this book we will explore some key biblical passages that are especially ill-treated in this discussion, ill-treated precisely by failing to give their context its due.

A DIFFICULT BALANCE

The unhappy truth is that Christians have often found the "word versus deed" balance difficult to set and maintain, especially over the last two centuries of American history.

Prior to the Civil War many American Christians had achieved a certain even-handedness in their understanding of "word versus deed." They were actively spreading the gospel across the expanding nation (word), but they were also committed to the social dimensions of their calling (deed). They spent themselves and their resources in the building of hospitals and orphanages; they embraced the bourgeoning Sunday school movement as a way of ministering to poor and disenfranchised children; strong abolitionist convictions and efforts flourished among them.

But as the nineteenth century unfolded, another trend was also developing. The growing encroachments of liberal theology continued to leach the theological substance from the gospel. As the authority and reliability of the Bible came under fire, core teachings of historic Christianity began to melt away. The supernatural claims of the gospel were repudiated or reinterpreted, leaving behind not much more than a social ethic. Hence the rise of the so-called social gospel in the mainline churches. The gospel, according to this line of revisionist thinking, was not about abstract theological affirmations or distant questions of history, much less pie-in-the-sky visions of the future. It was about demonstrating mercy and justice to one's fellow man in the here and now. Thus did the pendulum swing away from word to deed.

Reacting to this trend in the latter part of the nineteenth century, the rising fundamentalist movement set itself to champion the theological core of the Christian faith. These forebears of modern evangelicals stressed what they believed were the historic fundamentals of that faith, such things as the authority and trustworthiness of the Scriptures, the virgin birth of Jesus, his substitutionary atonement on the cross, his bodily resurrection from the grave, and his imminent return. At the center of it all they stressed the crucial importance of a personal response of faith to the verbal witness of the good news of the gospel.

Unfortunately, along with their faithfulness to the preached Word, many of these early fundamentalists made the mistake of deserting the social dimensions of the church's mission, not entirely, but to a degree that distinguished them from their theological forbears. Many of them simply abdicated social concerns to those they believed had forfeited the theological core of the gospel. In contrast to the

> Their task, as they saw it, was to rescue from this dying world as many souls as possible through the promulgation of the good news about Jesus.

liberal social gospel, theirs became what some have called a "lifeboat theology." Their task, as they saw it, was to rescue from this dying world as many souls as possible through the promulgation of the good news about Jesus. Thus did these early fundamentalists, in their neglect of the important social dimensions of the church's calling, shift the pendulum to the other extreme—away from deed to word.

In the early decades of the twentieth century the pendulum began to swing back toward a more biblical balance. By 1947 Carl F. H. Henry's book *The Uneasy Conscience of American Fundamentalism* signaled a new day, at least for evangelicals. In this book Henry chided his fellow fundamentalists/evangelicals (the terms were in many ways interchangeable at the time) for their blind spots and failures in the realm of social engagement, yet without denigrating the central role of the verbal witness. Other important voices chimed in, and as the twentieth century waxed and then began to wane, evangelical social (not to mention political) engagement developed anew. By the end of the twentieth century the old lifeboat theology had almost disappeared among evangelicals. They were showing promise of having rediscovered something of the balance between word and deed called for in Bible.

But even as the twentieth century was ending and a new century dawning, indications that the pendulum might be swinging again in the opposite direction began to appear. New voices and new trends emerged to emphasize the church's social responsibilities, often at the expense of its verbal witness. With the rise of so-called postmodernity, the cultural environment was shifting. A confidence in language came to be viewed as an outmoded feature of modernity. *Logocentric* (that is, being too word centered) became a derogatory term. Increasingly experience, actions, and images were valorized, while the verbal dimensions of the church's calling were played down or even disparaged. Rising generations of young Christians seemed to think that the verbal expression of the gospel could almost be dispensed with. They grew increasingly passionate about the mercy and justice dimensions of the church's calling, but they seemed ever more relaxed about, oblivious to, suspicious of, or even hostile toward the church's verbal witness. "Deeds, not creeds" became a familiar slogan.

> The gospel is inherently a *verbal* thing, and preaching the gospel is inherently a *verbal* behavior. If the gospel is to be preached at all, it must be put into words.

TODAY'S ENVIRONMENT

Such a quick survey of necessity fails the complex trends just described, but perhaps it can be allowed to serve our present point: it has been difficult through the years for the church to find and maintain its balance on the respective roles of word and deed in its mission. Over time the pendulum has sometimes swung too far in one direction or the other. It may be doing so again in our generation.

Ours is an environment highly susceptible to the mistaken notion that the church's verbal witness may be optional. The temptations of our day are seductive. Verbal behavior in general has fallen on hard postmodern times. The world will often applaud our feeding the hungry and healing the sick, but it will not applaud the word of the cross. The gospel of Jesus Christ represents a line in the sand. Jesus is the "stone of stumbling," the "rock of offense" who scandalizes the world (1 Pet. 2:6–8).

The sensibilities of our cultural moment thus combine with our natural inclination to avoid the stigma and rejection associated with Jesus. Together they conspire to shuttle us toward good deeds at the expense of gospel words. The result is inevitable: our verbal witness begins to suffer a benign neglect. We come to find comfort in the notion that our deeds matter more than our words; indeed, that our deeds can *substitute* for our words. Not to worry, we seem to say, we're preaching the gospel every day. We're just doing it with our actions.

This may be a comforting notion but it's also dangerously misleading. However important our actions may be (and, as we shall see, they are very important indeed), and whatever else they may be doing (which subject we will also explore), those actions are not "preaching the gospel." Despite the fact that so many today seem to think otherwise, one simply cannot preach the gospel without words. Let us say it again: the

21

gospel is inherently a *verbal* thing, and preaching the gospel is inherently a *verbal* behavior. If the gospel is to be preached at all, it must be put into words.

These are strong claims. They fly in the face of a good deal of current popular thinking. Can such claims stand the light of examination? We shall see, for an examination of these claims is precisely what follows.

THE IMPORTANCE
OF OUR WORDS

CHAPTER ONE

VERBAL AND NONVERBAL COMMUNICATION

We respond to gestures with an extreme alertness and, one might almost say, in accordance with an elaborate and secret code that is written nowhere, known to none, and understood by all.

—Edward Sapir, 1949

If we are to sort our way through the "word versus deed" debate, the first thing we require, even before we turn to the Scriptures, is an appropriate framework for our thinking, one that will help us make sense of the issues rather than confuse them. This chapter is designed to provide that framework.

The categories we require are these: *verbal communication* and *nonverbal communication*. We have been using the terms *word* and *deed*, and it will be immediately apparent that these correspond directly to the terms *verbal* and *nonverbal*. The difference in both cases focuses on whether we are using words.

Both verbal and nonverbal communication have been the subject of almost three millennia of fascinating and useful study, so we may ask ourselves what insights this work might contribute to our discussion. If we can pause for a moment and focus on this question, much of what follows will fall into place.

VERBAL VERSUS NONVERBAL

The term *verbal communication* refers to all those ways we communicate using a linguistic code. We call the various linguistic codes "languages." English, Spanish, Russian, Hindi, Japanese, Urdu, Swahili, Portuguese: all such languages are linguistic codes. Each of these codes has its own grammar, syntax, and vocabulary. These are the features we study when we try to master a new language.

Notice that the distinction here is not whether we are making sounds. That's *vocal* versus *nonvocal*. For instance, writing is a form of verbal behavior because it uses the verbal code, but it's soundless. Conversely, grunting is vocal (that is,

> Too often, the nonverbal component of interpersonal interchanges has received only passing reference or has been ignored entirely. Such oversight can lead to some erroneous conclusions about the interpersonal communication process.
> —Judee K. Burgoon

acoustically conveyed) but not verbal. The verbal/nonverbal distinction has to do not with whether we are making sounds but whether we are using a linguistic code (language, words) for our communication.

If verbal communication depends upon words, the term *nonverbal communication* refers to all those ways we communicate without words. Verbal codes are notoriously complicated, as anyone who has tried to learn a language can testify, but the nonverbal codes are in some ways still more complex. There are no books of formal grammar for the nonverbal codes; nor, most likely, can there ever be. The nonverbal dimensions of our communication are too subtle and contextual to be captured so concisely. They are supremely nuanced and difficult to master. That's why long after having mastered a new language, fluent speakers are often still giving off nonverbal miscues, picked up only by native speakers.

NONVERBAL COMMUNICATION

Humans communicate nonverbally in a variety of ways. We do not require for our purposes a detailed survey, but the following are some of the more obvious ways humans engage one another nonverbally:

- *Facial expression*: Think of a smile, a frown, a look of concentration, or contentment. The face is perhaps the most expressive part of the body, followed by the hands.

- *Gestures*: Waving, or pointing, or thrusting out the palm of the hand to halt someone are common nonverbal cues. Consider how effective speakers use gestures to enhance their messages. Some nationalities are known for "talking with their hands" while speaking. Others tend to limit their gestures.

- *Head position*: Head position tends to correlate with perceived status. Deference is communicated with a lowered head position, while a high head position communicates the reverse. Hence the notion of "looking down our nose" at someone.

- *Eye behavior*: Think of staring, rolling the eyes, winking, or refusing to make eye contact. Consider how subtly the eyes can express dreaminess, sadness, or interest.

- *Vocal inflection* (often called "paralanguage"): Imagine two husbands saying to their wives, "You look great." The one expresses himself enthusiastically, while the other uses a sarcastic "tone of voice." The contrasting vocal inflections enable the same three words to express opposite messages.

- *Touch behavior*: Touching, or the lack of it, tends to express relationship. The amount of touching, the location of the touch, the age and genders involved—these and many other touch factors communicate volumes.

- *Physical appearance and dress*: How we dress and groom ourselves communicate more than we realize. We are constantly reading one another's appearance. Studies show that the conclusions people draw about strangers, based solely on appearance, are often surprisingly uniform and accurate.

- *Posture*: The popular term *body language* includes several of the above dimensions, but posture is one of its key elements. Consider how one's body position can communicate confidence or fear, formality or informality, interest or indifference.

- *Use of space* (sometimes called "proxemics"): We often use space to express, for instance, our emotional connections to others. Think of the closeness that informs everyone a young couple is newly married, or the distant demeanor, the standoffishness, of strangers or enemies.

- *Surroundings*: Consider how much we quickly conclude about others when we catch a glimpse of the condition of their car, or their desktop, or their clothes closet. How we order our surroundings is one of the ways we communicate with those around us.

- *Actions*: We are constantly assessing one another on the basis of behavior. Actions are not self-contained; humans draw inferences about what they cannot see from the conduct they do see. We "read" other people's actions for their meaning, just as they do ours.

If verbal and nonverbal communication can be distinguished in theory, it's also true that in everyday practice they tend to occur in concert. And we are usually glad when they do. Writing typically strips out the nonverbal dimension, leaving us having to read between the lines for the information usually carried at the nonverbal level. Interestingly, in our digital age so-called emoticons—for example, :-) for happy;

:-(for sad; (*_*) for surprised—have been devised to off-set some of this loss. Telephone conversations enable some of the vocal inflection to come through, but all the visual cues are lacking. Video conferences or meetings using Internet services such as Skype add some of the visual information, especially facial expression, but even here many of the other nonverbal cues available in face-to-face settings are lacking. Typically our interpersonal communication works best when both the verbal and nonverbal codes are fully available to work together.

The relationship between the verbal and nonverbal dimensions of our communication is itself a fascinating and complicated subject. These two communication channels work together in a variety of important ways:

- *Repeating*: A woman forcefully points to the door and says, "Get out!" The nonverbal dimension of her communication is repeating the verbal dimension. Either might have stood on its own, but in combination her message is strengthened.

- *Complementing*: When a speaker, describing the open plain he had seen, uses wide gestures with his hands and arms, he is using a nonverbal channel to enhance the verbal. The broad gestures alone would convey little, but when combined with the verbal description the gestures serve a complementing function.

- *Substituting*: When asked if you will be attending the party you simply shrug your shoulders. You might have replied, "I'm not sure," but instead you allow this common nonverbal gesture to convey your meaning.

- *Contradicting*: We typically try to coordinate our verbal and nonverbal messages. You can experience this by trying a simple exercise: Say "yes" out loud while shaking your head "no." It requires a bit of concentration because we are so used to coordinating our verbal and nonverbal messages. But some-times the opposite occurs: our verbal and nonverbal messages contradict one another. For example, nervous gestures or tell-tale facial cues may alert us that someone is lying.

- *Regulating:* We often use nonverbal cues to regulate the flow of verbal communication. For instance, we may use eye behavior (catching someone's eye) to initiate the flow of verbal communication. Or we do the reverse: we use so-called exit cues (such as checking our watch) to terminate a conversation.

Human communication is an endlessly fascinating subject, and the verbal/nonverbal distinction is only one way of analyzing it. But these are the two categories that are most relevant to our present discussion. What can we learn from even this quick summary? The following insights are especially pertinent.

One cannot not *communicate.* We are constantly communicating with one another, if not verbally, then nonverbally. If we say, "I will simply remain still and say nothing," our very stillness and silence are communicating.

> The power of the nonverbal aspects of our interpersonal communication lies in their ability to express the affective dimension of our messages.

We tend to grant nonverbal messages more credence. When they contradict, we tend to believe nonverbal messages over verbal messages because the nonverbal dimensions of our communication are much more difficult to control. This is the working premise of lie detector tests. It's relatively easy for those attached to a lie detector (polygraph) machine to deceive with their words, but the nonverbal indicators the machine is measuring (blood pressure, heart rate, respiration, galvanic skin response) give them away. We can control our conscious words far more easily than we can control our often unconscious nonverbal messages, many of which we may not even be aware we are sending.

That's why when we must choose between conflicting messages, we tend to believe the nonverbal over the verbal. Hence the old adage, "Your actions speak so loud I can't hear what you say."

Nonverbal channels are especially effective in communicating attitudes, moods, feelings, and relationships. The power of the nonverbal aspects of our interpersonal communication lies in their ability to express the affective dimension of our messages. Whatever a speaker may be saying verbally, how she *feels* about her subject matter, or about her hearers, or even about herself is what tends to come across nonverbally. Without these sorts of affective cues, interpersonal messages often lack depth and dimension. But with them our communication achieves a greater richness. That's why when it's unavailable to us, as in reading a written message, we tend to feel the loss of the nonverbal dimension. We normally value and even depend upon the kinds of personal information nonverbal channels so effectively convey.

Nonverbal channels are inadequate for conveying cognitive content. If nonverbal channels are extremely effective in communicating moods, feelings, relationships, or attitudes, by the same token they are largely incapable of conveying cognitive, abstract, or historical information.

This is easily demonstrated. Imagine you have been assigned the task of communicating the following idea to a particular individual: Aristotle tutored Alexander the Great at the Macedonian court between 342 and c. 339 BC. Unfortunately, you discover that your pupil has no previous knowledge of either Aristotle or Alexander, what a tutor is, what Macedonia is, who Christ was, or consequently, what BC means. What's more, as if your task were not difficult enough, you do not have the verbal code available to you. Your pupil does not speak your language and you do not speak hers. In other words, you cannot use words to express your ideas. All you have available are nonverbal channels of communication. How would you go about your task?

You can see immediately that your assignment would be impossible. You cannot communicate this type of content nonverbally. What facial expressions, or gestures, or eye behavior, or actions could express information about Alexander or Macedonia? The nonverbal code is simply incapable of bearing this sort of content. What you require is the verbal code—words and sentences and paragraphs—to convey your meaning. Without them your task is not doable.

> Verbal behavior is neither unimportant nor dispensable. God's revelation came to us, after all, not only in the living Word, Jesus Christ, but in the written Word, the Scriptures.

But wait. Perhaps with enough time, one might say, you could use pictures, or perhaps mime, to communicate these ideas. But that won't work either. The more abstract the information, the more impossible your task. It would be a slog, but let us suppose you might eventually be able to use these channels to make slight progress in explaining what it means to be a tutor. But how could you ever explain who Aristotle was, or what BC means?

Mime artists intentionally forego the use of the verbal code, using only nonverbal channels to communicate their messages. But notice what they communicate and what they cannot communicate. Much of their art depends on the strengths of the nonverbal code (expressing sadness or happiness, for instance), and the rest depends on reminding observers, by acting, what the observers already know, either from experience or from what they have previously learned via the verbal code (e.g., in school). Without such props, not even the most gifted mime could explain to your pupil through actions alone who Aristotle was. Nonverbal channels cannot bear this kind of informational weight. Their usefulness lies elsewhere. If our goal is to express cognitive, abstract, or historical content, the verbal code is required. Words and sentences are simply indispensable.

INVALUABLE WORDS

We live in a day, as we have said, when the nonverbal dimensions of human communication (images, gestures, actions) are sometimes valorized at the expense of the verbal dimension. Visual media such as movies, YouTube, or video games are massively popular, while wordy endeavors such as poetry or newspapers have fallen on hard times. The tendency to trust and depend on language is sometimes denigrated, not seldom, we might note, by authors using words to do so.

Such critiques are not without their value. Yet Christians should resist acquiescing too quickly to these trends. Verbal behavior is neither unimportant nor dispensable. God's revelation came to us, after all, not only in the living Word, Jesus Christ, but in the written Word, the Scriptures. What's more, the use of the verbal code lies at the heart of what it means to be human, so much so that we can scarcely imagine life and society without it. We require language to speak of other people, places, and times (e.g., Aristotle, Alexander, ancient Greece); or to make statements that can be proven true or false ("My insurance company is the largest in the world"); or to express infinitely useful abstractions such as "chairs," "Democrats," "historians," or "polynomial equations." We use words to express the relative worth of something ("She makes the best coffee") or to describe the nature of something else ("Wheaton is a liberal arts college"). We use the verbal code to express policies ("Copies must be paid for in advance at the front desk") or to urge actions ("Jobs and employment should be the nation's first priority"). And most wonderful of all, each of these verbal functions can be combined to produce complex analyses, explanations, and arguments. The ability to use words lies at the center of what it means to be human. To devalue the one is to devalue the other.

So what does all of this mean for our "word versus deed" debate? Read on.

CHAPTER TWO

THE GOSPEL IS VERBAL

The gospel is not a concept that needs fresh ideas, but a story that needs fresh telling. It is the unchanged story of what God has done to save the world, supremely in the historical events of the life, death, resurrection, and reign of Jesus Christ.

—Preamble, "The Cape Town Commitment"

We have said that we cannot preach the gospel by our actions. The gospel can only be communicated with words. With the previous chapter's discussion in hand we are now in a position to see why.

A word of warning: I intend to belabor this point in what follows. My goal in this chapter is to put to rest once and for all the false notion that we can preach the gospel by our deeds; that is, that our actions can substitute for the verbal witness of the gospel. Why is this important? It's important because it is crucial that we remain clear about the unique complementary roles both our words *and* our deeds are designed to play in the mission of the church.

THE GOSPEL

In 1 Corinthians 15:1–8 the apostle Paul offers a summary of the gospel he had announced to the Corinthians. "I would remind you," he says, "of the gospel I preached to you." This is the gospel "which you received, in which you stand." It is

THE IMPORTANCE OF OUR WORDS

by this gospel "you are being saved, if you hold fast to the word I preached to you." This message was not Paul's own, he reminds them, in the sense that he had made it up or discovered it for himself. He had "received" it and then "delivered [it] to you as of first importance." Here is his summary of the content of that gospel:

> That Christ died for our sins in accordance with the Scriptures, that he was buried, that he was raised on the third day in accordance with the Scriptures, and that he appeared to Cephas, then to the twelve. Then he appeared to more than five hundred brothers at one time, most of whom are still alive, though some have fallen asleep. Then he appeared to James, then to all the apostles. Last of all, as to one untimely born, he appeared also to me.

If we accept this as a shorthand summary of the gospel, it becomes immediately apparent that it is impossible to communicate such a message nonverbally. One could no more communicate these ideas nonverbally than one could communicate our message about Aristotle nonverbally. The cognitive content of the message renders this an impossibility. The biblical gospel is inherently a *verbal* thing, and communicating it by definition requires *verbal* behavior.

JESUS AND HIS APOSTLES

But what if one is not willing to grant that the above is a valid summary of the gospel? This may be what we hear from the apostle Paul, a critic might object, but when we turn to the life of Jesus as reported in the Gospels, the picture appears quite different. Jesus's ministry was more holistic. He went about feeding the hungry and healing the sick. Paul's summary of the gospel is a partial and diminished thing from a secondary source. We must give priority to Jesus as the author of our faith and follow his model of preaching the gospel with our deeds as well as our words.

Various versions of this objection have been around for a long while—we think of such disparate figures as F. C. Bauer, Friedrich Nietzsche, Ernest Renan or George Bernard Shaw—and they can still be heard today. We will return to the question of the appropriate *content* of the gospel in a later chapter, but in the meantime let us focus on two preliminary responses to this objection, the first being that it is based on an unfortunate disjunction between Jesus and Paul.

The term *apostle* stems from the Greek verb *apostello*, which means "to send." Apostles are those who are sent by someone; they are "sent ones." In our case the New Testament apostles were chosen, trained, authorized, empowered, and sent by no less than Jesus himself. This is what makes it so misleading to set Paul over against Jesus. This issue pops up so often throughout the "word versus deed" discussion that it's worth exploring for a moment.

The Apostles. Consider this testimony from the New Testament: Jesus handpicked his apostles and then trained them over a period of years. As he neared his death, he began to instruct them about what to expect. After I'm gone, he said, "I will ask the Father, and he will give you another Helper, to be with you forever, even the Spirit of truth. . . . You know him, for he dwells with you and will be in you" (John 14:16–17). Once that happens, Jesus said, "the Helper, the Holy Spirit, whom the Father will send in my name, he will teach you all things and bring to your remembrance all that I have said to you" (v. 26). "When the Helper comes, whom I will send to you from the Father, the Spirit of truth, who proceeds from the Father, he will bear witness about me" (John 15:26). He is the one who, when he comes, "will guide you into all the truth" (John 16:13).

After his death and resurrection, Jesus appeared to these

same men and provided them further instructions. "I am sending the promise of my Father upon you. But stay in the city until you are clothed with power from on high" (Luke 24:49). "He ordered them not to depart from Jerusalem, but to wait for the promise of the Father, which, he said, "you heard from me; for John baptized with water, but you will be baptized with the Holy Spirit not many days from now. . . . But you will receive power when the Holy Spirit has come upon you, and you will be my witnesses in Jerusalem and in all Judea and Samaria, and to the end of the earth" (Acts 1:4–8).

Immediately upon delivering these instructions Jesus was taken up into heaven "before their very eyes" (v. 9 NIV). A few days later, on the day of Pentecost, the Father fulfilled his promise by pouring out his Spirit upon the world in a way that world had never experienced. The Spirit had always been present in the world, but never before like this. Pentecost represented a paradigm shift in the Spirit's relationship to God's people.

The crowds in Jerusalem were astonished by this dramatic development, and the newly empowered apostles used the opportunity to preach the gospel. Where a few weeks before these were a small band of despondent and defeated disciples, with their fresh imbuement of the Spirit the apostles proved themselves to be courageous witnesses, explaining to the crowd the supernatural phenomena they were experiencing. This Jesus whom you recently crucified, Peter proclaimed, "was not abandoned to Hades, nor did his flesh see corruption. This Jesus God raised up, and of that we all are witnesses. Being therefore exalted at the right hand of God, and having received from the Father the promise of the Holy Spirit, he has poured out this that you yourselves are seeing and hearing" (Acts 2:31–33).

This was the beginning of the church's role as the new temple, God's earthly dwelling place not built with human hands (Acts 17:24). The risen Christ sent out his apostles to build that temple (1 Cor. 3:16; 2 Cor. 6:16). If Jesus was to be its cornerstone, the apostles were assigned to lay its foundation; indeed, they were to *be* that foundation (Eph. 2:20–21; see also 1 Cor. 12:28). By the power of the newly imparted Spirit, who would guide them in all truth and remind them of everything he had taught them, Jesus would direct the work and the words of these apostles. Through their Spirit-empowered preaching, teaching, and writing, the risen Head of the church would direct his body. This is what is meant by the term *apostolic authority*. These men carried the unique authority of Jesus himself.

Officers of Jesus. Karl Heinrich Rengstorf was probably the twentieth century's leading authority on the subject of apostleship in the New Testament.[1] Said he, "By the commission of Jesus a number of men, especially those who were closest to Him during His life, became his representatives in the sense that they took his place, and thus assumed an authoritative position in the little company of Christians."[2]

According to Rengstorf, the entire basis of the New Testament apostleship is "the will and commission of the risen Lord."[3] This team of insignificant men, joined by Paul after the death of Jesus, was formed on the initiative of Jesus and became his fellow workers (Matt. 10:1; Mark 6:7; Luke 9:1). They were not, as were the later elders or deacons, officials of the congregation; they were uniquely officers of Jesus himself. Their commission as bearers of the New Testament message came directly from him, and he used them to build his body. By displaying his power through them, in both their words and actions, Jesus gave them his endorsement as his fully accredited representatives. The apostles were empowered to speak and act on his behalf. When they wrote or preached authoritatively as apostles, what they said to the church, the risen Christ, the head of the church (Col. 1:18), was saying to the church through them.

It's not difficult, then, to see why playing Paul off against Jesus is such a mistake. To do so calls into question the very foundation of apostolic authority, which in turn calls into question the edifice built upon that foundation, the church. This mistake fails to recognize that under the direction of the Holy Spirit, the gospel Paul preached was precisely the gospel that the risen, exalted Christ was empowering him to preach; indeed, it was the gospel Jesus himself was preaching through his spokesman Paul. The apostle's summary of the gospel is Christ's summary of the gospel. To discount the one is to discount the other.

Important Differences. Notice that these claims of apostolic authority do not require us to claim there were no differences between the message we find Jesus preaching in the Gospels and the message Paul preached to his audiences. On the contrary, we should be surprised if there were no differences. All of Jesus's public teaching predated his death, resurrection, ascension, and exaltation, not to mention the Father's outpouring of the Spirit in a new way and the initiation of the church. Such dramatic developments in the progress of revelation could scarcely help but generate differences.[4] These momentous events prompted major and immediate developments in the apostolic message, as can be seen in Peter's Pentecostal sermon in Acts 2. Peter's message there is strikingly different from anything he could have preached even two months earlier. That Paul's and Jesus's messages should show equally significant differences is hardly surprising. Yet they were differences generated by the new developments, not by some alleged disjunction between Jesus and his apostle.

What is surprising, however—unless we're ready to jettison the notion of apostolic authority—is the charge that Paul's message was somehow inferior and secondary, much less contradictory, to that of Jesus. Such a charge flies in the face of Christ's stated commission for his "sent ones," his apostles, and for that particular apostle named Paul. There is a God, and he is not silent. "Long ago, at many times and in many ways, God spoke to our fathers by the prophets, but in these last days he has spoken to us by his Son" (Heb. 1:1–2). The Son in turn appointed and empowered his apostles to speak on his behalf: "Paul, an apostle—not from men nor through man, but through Jesus Christ and God the Father" (Gal. 1:1; see also Acts 9:15). This was Christ's own plan for building his church.

Paul and Jesus cannot be played off against one another without doing a disservice to one or both. Paul was an extension of the one he served. What he preached was the message the risen Christ called him to preach; in fact, it was the message the risen, exalted Jesus himself was preaching through his handpicked, personally commissioned, Spirit-empowered apostle.

MISTAKEN STRATEGIES

Even if we were to conclude that Jesus was not speaking through Paul, however, and that Paul's gospel was somehow inferior to Christ's, our observation that the gospel cannot be preached without words would stand. We have been discussing the relationship between Jesus and Paul, but however we decide that question, what is certain is that in both cases their respective messages were of the sort that demand the verbal code. If Paul's message could not be preached without words, neither could Jesus's message: "Repent, for the kingdom of heaven is at hand" (Matt. 4:17). Any such message, not to mention its elaboration, required the verbal code no less than Paul's.

Neither Jesus nor any of his apostles ever "preached the gospel" by their actions, nor could they. There is both a carelessness of thought and sloppiness of language inherent in the claim that we can preach the gospel without words. Such a claim requires either that the gospel be emptied of its cognitive information or that we equivocate in our use of the term *preach*. But both of these strategies lead to confusion.

The Cognitive Content of the Gospel. The biblical idea of faith has long been understood to encompass three important dimensions: *notitia, assensus,* and *fiducia. Assensus* (assent) and *fiducia* (trust) are essential to faith, but so also is *notitia* (knowledge).

Knowledge does not save, but neither is biblical faith the proverbial "leap in the dark." The messages we hear from both Jesus and the apostles uniformly include cognitive information, content of the sort which, if it is to be known and communicated to another, requires the use of the verbal code. This point is scarcely debatable, as the examination of every biblical instance amply demonstrates. Deeds in and of themselves are never said to "preach" anything in the New Testament. Wherever something is said to be "preached," that something is always verbal content. Sometimes the content is simply labeled:

- The word.
- The word of God.
- The word of the Lord.
- The word of faith.
- The gospel.
- The gospel of the kingdom.
- Good news.
- Good news of good things.

In other places aspects of the verbal content are specified:

- "The word of the cross." (1 Cor. 1:18)
- "Christ crucified." (1 Cor. 1:23)
- "The unsearchable riches of Christ." (Eph. 3:8)
- "Jesus and the resurrection." (Acts 17:18)
- "Good news about the kingdom of God and the name of Jesus Christ." (Acts 8:12)

- "They should repent and turn to God, performing deeds in keeping with their repentance." (Acts 26:20)
- "Christ has been raised from the dead." (1 Cor. 15:20)
- "Through Jesus the forgiveness of sins is proclaimed to you." (Acts 13:38 NIV)
- "It was necessary for the Christ to suffer and to rise from the dead." (Acts 17:3)
- "They should repent." (Acts 26:20)
- "You should turn from these vain things to a living God, who made the heaven and the earth and the sea and all that is in them." (Acts 14:15)
- "He is the one appointed by God to be judge of the living and the dead." (Acts 10:42)
- "Repentance and forgiveness of sins should be proclaimed in his name to all nations." (Luke 24:47)
- "Peace to you who were far off and peace to those who were near." (Eph. 2:17)

In still other passages some of the verbal content is included:

- "This Jesus, whom I proclaim to you, is the Christ." (Acts 17:3)
- "The word is near you, in your mouth and in your heart." (Rom. 10:8)
- "Repent, for the kingdom of heaven is at hand." (Matt. 3:2)

In every instance, however, preaching in the New Testament involves verbal behavior. No one is ever said to "preach" anything, much less the gospel, via their deeds. The messages preached by Jesus and the apostles invariably involved content that could be conveyed only with words.

The Verbs for Preaching. Fudging on what we mean by "preach" doesn't help either. We might be tempted to try salvaging the notion of "preaching the gospel by our deeds" by claiming that we are speaking figuratively. Let us acknowledge, we might say, that we do not *literally* preach the gospel with our actions. But we can—what? What other verb might we choose? "Communicate" the gospel by our deeds? "Express" the gospel by our deeds? This is what I mean by a carelessness of thought and sloppiness of language. Whatever verb we choose, if the thought is that we are conveying the gospel message to another person by our actions, we are deceiving ourselves.

This is not to suggest, of course, that our actions communicate nothing. In the previous chapter we stressed the opposite; that is, our actions inevitably do communicate, and, in fact, we cannot *avoid* communicating by our actions, for good or ill. But what these actions communicate cannot be "the gospel." Our actions can express many things. They can communicate how we *feel* about the gospel, or our attitude toward our listeners, or whether we are someone they should be willing to listen to. But communicating the gospel itself requires words and sentences and paragraphs.

This point is vividly and decisively demonstrated by the Greek verbs we translate as "preaching" in the New Testament. The two most common are *euaggelizo* ("to proclaim good news") and *kerusso* ("to announce as a herald"), and both denote verbal behavior. Never in the New Testament are these verbs used figuratively of nonverbal behavior. These are joined by other speaking verbs—*kataggello, martureo, parakaleo,* and *laleo*—which together reinforce the oral nature of the event.[5] The contexts consistently make clear that the behavior being described is verbal:

- "Proclaiming with a loud voice . . . " (Rev. 5:2)
- "What you have whispered in private rooms shall be proclaimed on the housetops." (Luke 12:3)
- "How are they to hear without someone preaching?" (Rom. 10:14)
- "Then Philip opened his mouth, and beginning with this Scripture he told him the good news about Jesus." (Acts 8:35)
- "For good news came to us just as to them, but the message they heard . . . " (Heb. 4:2)
- ". . . so that through me the message might be fully proclaimed and all the Gentiles might hear it." (2 Tim. 4:17)

CONCLUSION

So let us put this misleading way of speaking (and hence, thinking) to bed once and for all. The evidence is clear and unequivocal. The notion of preaching the gospel with our deeds is foreign to the Bible. Whenever we find there the gospel being "preached," it is always being communicated verbally, sometimes in explicit contrast to nonverbal behavior: "The blind receive their sight and the lame walk, lepers are cleansed and the deaf hear, and the dead are raised up, and the poor have good news preached to them" (Matt. 11:5; see also Matt. 4:23; 9:35; Luke 4:18; 7:22; 9:6). Nowhere does the Bible encourage us to think that our actions can stand in for our verbal witness. The gospel simply cannot be preached by our deeds. [6]

We have belabored this point for a reason—not because we wish to diminish the importance of our deeds; in later chapters I will stress their importance. But it is all-important that we keep clear *the respective roles* of our verbal and nonverbal witness. How we permit ourselves to talk about these issues shapes and/or reflects how we think about them, and how we think about them in turn shapes how we behave. If we permit ourselves to speak in a way that confuses important distinctions, we should not be surprised to see our carelessness show itself in equally confused behavior.

The stakes in thinking clearly about these issues are just this high. Obscuring or conflating the respective roles of word and deed can have serious consequences, as we will see in the following chapter.

CHAPTER THREE

EVANGELISM IS VERBAL

> Evangelism is the most basic and radical ministry possible to a human being. This is true not because the spiritual is more important than the physical, but because the eternal is more important than the temporal.
>
> —Tim Keller

Evangelism in the New Testament is not everything; it is one specific thing. It is the act of giving verbal witness to the gospel, the good news of Jesus Christ. As such, evangelism is inherently a verbal behavior. The act of evangelism is the act of communicating the gospel in words to others. This definition of evangelism, too, is a point we must keep clear and focused.

> To call sociopolitical liberation "salvation" and to call social activism "evangelism"—this is to be guilty of a gross theological confusion.
> —John Stott

God's mission for the church in the world retains evangelism at its center. But this mission also extends beyond that center. Evangelism is *one* of the tasks of the church, perhaps even, as Charles Malik once put it, the "first task" of the church.[1] But it is not the church's *only* task. If God's people are called to give verbal witness in the world, they are also called to a wide range of nonverbal tasks.

It is therefore a serious category error to collapse the church's full mission into the term *evangelism*, as is all too commonly done. Evangelism is not the entire mission of the church; hence the term should not be broadened to denote the whole. Doing so exposes us to at least three befuddling mistakes.

ALLOWING THE VERBAL WITNESS TO BE ECLIPSED

First, when we begin to think of the entire mission of the church as evangelism, the true act of evangelism—giving verbal witness to the gospel—is too easily crowded out. As we have noted, the nonverbal dimensions of the church's calling often find the world's approval and encouragement; such activism may well be applauded. But as Jesus warned and his church has consistently experienced over the centuries, this is seldom the reception that the church's verbal witness receives. Far more common has been the reception Paul experienced in Thessalonika.

To the Thessalonian church Paul was later able to say, "We . . . thank God constantly for this, that when you received the word of God, which you heard from us, you accepted it not as the word of men but as what it really is, the word of God" (1 Thess. 2:13). Yet this was scarcely the reception that same word received from the broader Thessalonian community (Acts 17:1–9). Both the apostle and the new believers there suffered grievously for their verbal witness (1 Thess. 1:8–10; 2:14–16). Why? As Paul observed to the Corinthians, while the good news of Jesus Christ is the very "power of God and the wisdom of God" to believers, it's also "a stumbling block to Jews and folly to Gentiles" (1 Cor. 1:24, 23). Hence those who bring this gospel message commonly receive a mixed response. They are "the aroma of Christ to God among those who are being saved and among those who are perishing, to one a fragrance from death to death, to the other a fragrance from life to life. Who is sufficient for these things?" (2 Cor. 2:15–16).

We in the West live in a generation that is allergic to almost any truth claims, much less the scandalous, all-encompassing claims the gospel makes for Jesus Christ. Ours is a time when language itself is devalued. Our culture has become skeptical about words. Images, experiences, and actions hold the high ground. In such times the verbal witness of the church is likely to carry a special stigma. The world may well affirm the church's efforts to help the poor or release the oppressed. But we will be disappointed if we expect the world to applaud the "word of the cross." The vast truth claims inherent in that word cut against the cultural grain, exacerbating the already inherent human tendency to resist the truth (Rom. 1:18ff.). As in every other generation, the verbal witness of the church in our day will likely be resisted by the culture. The gospel we proclaim may be the "fragrance of life" to believers, but we should not be surprised to find it has a very different aroma to others.

> Evangelism is not everything, and everything is not evangelism. Evangelism is its own unique thing, which nothing else can replace.

In such an environment, then, using the term *evangelism* to encompass the entire mission of the church makes it all too easy to abandon our verbal witness. It enables us to gravitate toward those parts of our calling that receive cultural approval while shying away from the part that generates cultural censure—all without abandoning "evangelism." We still care about evangelism, we assure ourselves, but we are evangelizing with our deeds rather than our words. Thus does our broadened definition enable us to deceive ourselves.

It is important to keep our definition of evangelism clear and biblically focused. Evangelism is not everything the church is called to do; it's a very particular thing. It is the act of giving verbal witness to the gospel, the good news of Jesus Christ. When the church is faithful in maintaining this verbal witness, its mission is scarcely exhausted. But, likewise, however faithful we may be in fulfilling the other dimensions of our mission, none can substitute for evangelism. Evangelism is not everything, and everything is not evangelism. Evangelism is its own unique thing, which nothing else can replace.

Keeping this point uncluttered will help us avoid the self-deception inherent in the illusion that we are preaching the gospel with our deeds. If we are foolish enough, or cowardly enough, to abandon our verbal witness due to social pressure, let us at least resist deluding ourselves, through the use of obfuscating language, that we are still doing evangelism. Let us be honest enough to acknowledge that we are vacating our verbal witness, however faithful we may be to the nonverbal dimensions of our calling. This is preferable to deceiving ourselves by defining our failure away. Better yet, let us be clear about the verbal *and* nonverbal dimensions of Christ's calling and remain faithful to both.

MISPLACING THE POWER

We must keep our understanding of evangelism clear for a second reason. It will help us avoid any mistaken notions about where the power lies. If the gospel is powerful—which the Bible assures us it is—its power resides not in us but in the gospel itself. This crucial insight also appears to be underappreciated in our time, but it needs to be recovered.

God's Word in general is uniformly portrayed in the Bible as powerful. But here we are interested in that peculiar word we know as "the gospel." According to the Scriptures, this word possesses a unique salvific power, a point which is easily lost if we broaden the term *evangelism* to refer to both the verbal *and* nonverbal dimensions of our calling.

Some time ago I was asked to provide a public response to a paper written by a well-known author and pastor. The paper attempted to lay out a new evangelistic strategy attuned to our postmodern times. It was a thoughtful paper containing many insights I not only agreed with but had been championing for years. But it also fell into the very confusion we are discussing here.

The paper consistently played down the church's verbal witness in favor of its deeds, an argument in which the above postmodern tendencies played a featured role. But more to our present point, in pressing for a holistic vision of the church's mission—a crucial biblical emphasis—the author proceeded to call for a redefinition of evangelism, one that included what we have been referring to as the "nonverbal dimensions" of our calling. "There is no true evangelism," he said, "without embodied action." In fact, if this fuller view of things does not catch on, he continued, we should be pessimistic about the prospects for evangelism in our contemporary world. "Unless [Christ's] disciples are following the Great Commandment [love for God and neighbor], it is fruitless to engage in the Great Commission."

> Nothing hinders evangelism today more than
> the widespread loss of confidence in the truth,
> relevance and power of the gospel.
> —John Stott

It is astonishing how often we hear such sentiments expressed these days, just this baldly. According to this view, the gospel is without its own potency. It is hollow and powerless, it seems, without us. The power of the gospel lies not in the Spirit's convicting application of the message to human hearts but in us its messengers, so much so that if we fail to be and do all that we should, our evangelistic efforts will prove fruitless.

But this is not the testimony of the New Testament. According to the apostle Paul, the power of the gospel does not reside in us; it resides in the Spirit's application of the gospel message itself. "I am not ashamed of the gospel," Paul said. Why? Because "it" — the verbal gospel, the "word of the cross," the good news of Jesus Christ — is "the power of God for salvation" to everyone who believes (Rom. 1:16).

Can we allow this bold apostolic affirmation to sink in, and then embrace it? It is not our lives, however well lived, that render the gospel powerful. It is not the church's faithfulness in fulfilling its holistic mission that provides the gospel its potency. The good news of Jesus Christ displays its own Spirit-driven power quite apart from us. It is "the word of the cross" itself, says Paul to the Corinthians, that "is the power of God" (1 Cor. 1:18).

So strong was Paul's confidence in the gospel's inherent Spirit-infused power that he could rejoice even when it was being preached not merely in the absence of "embodied action," but out of overtly sinful motives:

> I want you to know, brothers, that what has happened to me has really served to advance the gospel, so that it has become known throughout the whole imperial guard and to all the rest that my imprisonment is for Christ. And most of the brothers, having become confident in the Lord by my imprisonment, are much more bold to speak the word without fear. Some indeed preach Christ from envy and rivalry, but others from good will. The latter do it out of love, knowing that I am put here for the defense of the gospel. The former proclaim Christ out of selfish ambition, not sincerely but thinking to afflict me in my imprisonment. What then? Only

that in every way, whether in pretense or in truth, Christ is proclaimed, and in that I rejoice. (Phil. 1:12–18)

If the call to redefine evangelism were on target, by these standards the ministry of the greatest evangelist of all times, Christ's handpicked apostle to the Gentiles, must be deemed a failure. Paul's itinerant ministry as a herald met few of the "embodied action" criteria. It thus becomes a deadly model for today; in fact, it represents virtually the antithesis to what this leader says is required. Paul's confidence was in the power of the message of the cross to save—a message he typically delivered on the move from place to place to strangers who knew relatively little of the unimpressive messenger. Was his confidence misplaced? Surely not. Neither Paul's method nor his message was mistaken. Both were assigned directly by Jesus himself.

We must not allow the disarray of our generation to confuse us about our own core issues, which is what happens when we draw this broad and holistic vision of what God calls his church to be and do into the very definition of evangelism itself. It is a serious category error to confuse the whole of what God calls the church to do with one of its parts. This leads to the false conclusion that if the church falls short in the fulfillment of this holistic vision, as it always has done, its evangelistic efforts will inevitably prove "fruitless."

When, we must ask, has the church been all it should be? When, short of glory, will the church ever *be* all that God wills for it? The church has been from the beginning a messy affair, falling far short of living out the Great Commandment. Thus it has been, and, sadly, given our human sinfulness, thus it is likely always to be. But thankfully, the spiritual power of the gospel is not held hostage to our shortcomings. Despite our failures, the gospel itself remains marvelously potent, the very "power of God for salvation" to them that believe.

Few would deny—certainly not me!—that the holistic

mission of the church is the best possible platform for the church's verbal witness and that our jaded generation will be more inclined to give us a hearing if we are living it out. I have argued this very point repeatedly elsewhere and I will stress it again later in this book. But this does not permit us to reverse the equation by making evangelism itself coterminous with that broader vision and then concluding that the efficacy of the gospel lies captive to our faithfulness in fulfilling it. When evangelism is made to be everything, then it is no longer that one thing, that focused thing the New Testament consistently shows it to be. This is a prescription for a loss of vision for, and confidence in, the verbal witness of the gospel.

> If we confuse evangelism and social justice we lose what is the single most unique service that Christians can offer the world. Others, alongside believers, can feed the hungry. But Christians have the gospel of Jesus by which men and women can be born again into the certain hope of eternal life.
> —Tim Keller

It is the height of human presumption to conclude that the power of the gospel lies somehow in us, so much so that if we fail, the gospel itself is disabled and rendered impotent. We must resist our sinful bent toward this presumption in order to remain clear about where the true power resides. The gospel's potency lies not in the messenger, however faithfully we may be fulfilling our calling. It lies in the intent of the Spirit to use the gospel to bring men and women to God.

Let us keep our thinking clear: it is the gospel, the word of the cross that is the power of God for salvation. And evangelism, if we are to speak biblically, is the heralding of that good news to all who will listen. If many within our generation prove unwilling to hear that good news, they will not be the first to do so. Perhaps, like Isaiah's generation, their hearing of God's truth will only drive them deeper into their unbelief. Yet even if this turns out to be the case, we must not allow that cultural reality to confuse our understanding of the evangelistic task or undermine our confidence in the gospel's power to do its work.

Evangelism is the act of giving verbal witness to the good news of Jesus Christ, confident that its power does not fluctuate with the strengths or weaknesses of the messengers. This is a humbling truth but also immensely liberating. In the end, my inability to answer objections, my lack of training or experience, even failures in my own faithfulness in living it out, do not nullify the gospel's power. Its potency is an intrinsic thing due to the working of God's Spirit. The sobering and liberating truth is that *even at our best* the gospel is powerful in spite of us, not because of us. Thanks be to God.

MISUNDERSTANDING GOD'S METHODS

The third reason we must guard against broadening our definition of evangelism is that it will help us remain clear about how God has chosen to work in the world, and why. He has elected to work through our verbal witness for a very important reason, one often overlooked in our time. He has chosen this modus operandi precisely "so that no human being might boast in the presence of God" (1 Cor. 1:29).

In 1 Corinthians 1:21 the apostle Paul says, "For since, in the wisdom of God, the world did not know God through wisdom, it pleased God through *the folly of what we preach* to save those who believe." Paul is referring here to what we have been calling the "verbal witness" of the gospel.

What is it about this verbal witness that Paul says is foolish? Is it the *content*—the odd notion of the world being salvaged through "a certain Jesus, who was dead, but whom Paul asserted to be alive" (Acts 25:19)—or its *form*, a message not powerfully argued but simply announced as a herald? A careful study of this crucial passage indicates that it is both.[2]

Paul's assumption throughout this passage—indeed, throughout all of his writings—is that the human race is lost in its sin. It desperately needs to be rescued from the judgment of the Creator against whom it has mutinied. But human pride, as always, is the great barrier. Humans are convinced that if only they apply themselves, they can solve this dilemma on their own.

This was the notion Paul sought to put to rest. When it comes to solving this most pressing of all human problems, "where is the one who is wise?," he asks. "Where is the scribe? Where is the debater of this age?" (1 Cor. 1:20). Whatever else their vaunted wisdom might accomplish, has not God made foolish all of their feeble attempts to solve *this problem* on their own? The world may be impressed by the prideful efforts of its best and brightest to scale the heights and achieve for themselves eternal life; indeed, to come to know the divine, even to *become* the divine. But God himself will have none of it. In his sovereign wisdom he has cut off this approach. Humans simply cannot and will not solve their dilemma in their own strength. If they are to come to God at all, Paul says, they must do so on God's terms.

And God's terms are these: he will provide the race with an avenue of salvation, but it will be available only through means that run profoundly *contrary* to human pride. To discover this salvation men and women will have to renounce their pretensions to self-sufficiency, acknowledge their helplessness, and give up striving to save themselves. They must humble themselves before God by acknowledging a crucified Jewish peasant as Lord of the universe and his death on a cross as their only hope of salvation. They must trust him and him alone as their only means of salvation.

Worse yet, God will not tolerate any lingering pride. Humans must be willing to place their faith in Jesus solely on the basis of hearing and accepting God's *announced word* on the subject, the gospel. He will not satisfy their pride in other ways. If they demand miraculous signs to authenticate the announcement, God will not provide them. If they insist on something more along the lines of what the Greeks required to be impressed—"wisdom" in the form of convincing arguments designed to satisfy self-sufficient minds, all dressed in winsomely impressive language—he will not provide this either. All they will receive is the simple declaration of the gospel by God's faithful heralds. As Jesus himself often put it, "He who has ears to hear, let him hear."

No doubt Paul understood that many in his audience, to the extent they were unwilling to renounce their pride, would find this announcement absurdly unsatisfying. The typical Jew, he says, would be scandalized by it, while the typical Greek would disdain it as ridiculous. In their vanity they are unwilling to identify themselves with such a low-status salvation, because they are unwilling to accept that they must be reduced to such a humble estate.

> By the standards of the world the message of Christ crucified is indeed a foolish message. But it is important to see that this content is not the only thing that lacks standing in the eyes of the world.

But God knew from the beginning what he was doing. He might have come to the race through its own striving, but he knew that, in the end, humans would proudly claim credit for their salvation. Instead, God intentionally chose to make himself available through means the proud would find unacceptable—that is, through means which repudiate all human pretensions and allow only the humble acceptance of a simply announced, crucified Christ—so that, in the end, it would be clear that God alone was responsible for salvation. No mortal could boast (1 Cor. 1:27–29).

This is the argument that forms the context of 1 Corinthians 1:21. When Paul speaks of "the folly of what we preach," he intends his reader to understand more than its content alone. To be sure, Paul is referring here to the content of the preaching. By the world's standards the message of Christ crucified is indeed a foolish message. But it is important to see that this content is not the only thing that lacks standing in the eyes of the world. When hearers want and expect to hear persuasive argumentation couched in impressive terms—in fact, *demand* it if they are to be impressed—the simple heralding of a declarative message will be greeted with derision. Along with the content, this form too will appear paltry and foolish by comparison, so much so that it will insult them. It will offend the worldling's pride and seem demeaning to him that he should be expected simply to *accept* the message as announced, on the mere say-so of its source.

This prideful stance, Paul argues, is what makes not only the *content* of the verbal witness unpalatable but also its *form*. In hearing the message of God's herald, the listener is dethroned from his proud role as judge. Far from gratifying his pride, the hearer is called simply to accept the message as proffered. To those who recognize their need and are willing to relinquish their pride, this proffered word, the word of the cross, appears to be the most astonishing and welcome "good news"; they bow to it willingly. But this the prideful are unwilling to do. If the content of the gospel, Christ crucified, is considered scandalous or foolish by the world's standards, so also will be its mere announcing.

None of this takes God by surprise, of course; it is all very much by his design. It pleased God, says Paul, through the foolishness of both the *content* and the *form* of the verbal witness to save those who simply believe. This humble response is all God asks—indeed, all he will accept. But any such kneeling in humility, repentance, and submission is a tall order for the proud.

> At that time Jesus declared, "I thank you, Father, Lord of heaven and earth, that you have hidden these things from the wise and understanding and revealed them to little children; yes, Father, for such was your gracious will."
> —Matthew 11:25–26

Jesus said, "As Moses lifted up the serpent in the wilderness, so must the Son of Man be lifted up, that whoever believes in him may have eternal life" (John 3:14–15). Later he claimed that when he was "lifted up from the earth" he would draw all people to himself (John 12:32). The apostle John explained, "He said this to show by what kind of death he was going to die" (v. 33), lifted up as a public spectacle on the cross, drawing to himself all who were willing to look upon him in faith for healing. Our verbal witness to Jesus continues that process of lifting Jesus up. "It was before your eyes that Jesus Christ was publicly portrayed as crucified," Paul says of his preaching to the Galatians (3:1). By our verbal witness we "placard" the crucified, risen Christ, displaying him for all to see, so that he, by his Spirit, might continue to draw men and women to himself. [3]

The church's evangelism thus plays a crucial role in God's chosen modus operandi in the world. Evangelism is the act of announcing verbally the good news of Jesus, lifting him up before the eyes of our generation, and it is essential that we keep this clear. Redefining evangelism so as to obscure or depreciate this verbal witness can only place us out of step with how God has chosen to operate in the world.

CONCLUSION

As always, we dwell in our generation as "sojourners and exiles" (1 Pet. 2:11). Moreover, we are to work hard at modeling for the world that *shalom* God intended for his creation. But let us avoid confusing this larger vision with the more specific task of evangelism, lest this narrower task be held hostage to our failure to fulfill the broader one.

Let us celebrate instead the reality that the power of the gospel resides not in us but in the Spirit's application of the message we proclaim, the message which displays a crucified Lord and Savior. Let us rejoice in the awareness that, as water is relevant to thirst, as food is relevant to hunger, as medicine is relevant to sickness, so this message, the truth that in Christ "God was reconciling the world to himself, not counting their trespasses against them" (2 Cor. 5:19), is relevant to the deepest and most profound need of every human heart, whatever their generation. And may we never lose heart in giving voice to it.

PART 2

THE IMPORTANCE OF OUR DEEDS

CHAPTER FOUR

ABSTRACTIONS AND THEIR USES

The interesting writer, the informative speaker, the accurate thinker . . . operate on all levels of the abstraction ladder, moving quickly and gracefully and in orderly fashion from the higher to the lower, from lower to higher, with minds as lithe and deft and beautiful as monkeys in a tree.

—S. I. Hayakawa

We stressed throughout the first section of this book that the gospel is a verbal thing. It cannot be "preached" nonverbally. If it is to be communicated at all, the gospel must be put into words. This is the very definition of evangelism.

But this leads inevitably to a second critical observation: giving verbal witness to the gospel does not *exhaust* the church's mission. Living faithfully for Christ involves not only our words, crucial though they may be; it also involves our actions. There is a *nonverbal* dimension to the church's mission as surely as there is a *verbal* dimension. What is this nonverbal dimension, and how does it relate to the verbal? These are the questions that will occupy us in Part 2.

To help us think through the Bible's answer to these questions, let us begin by establishing a second framework for our thinking. Like our earlier discussion of *verbal* and *nonverbal* behavior, this framework is drawn from the field of communication. The insights we are after are nicely summed up in what has come to be known as *the ladder of abstraction*.

THE ABSTRACTION LADDER

The discipline of general semantics was founded by the Polish-born scholar Alfred Korzybski (1879–1950). Korzybski was fascinated by the way humans think and use language. He focused in particular on the process of abstraction. His later followers, most notably a California university professor (and later US senator) named S. I. Hayakawa, popularized what came to be known as the ladder of abstraction.

THE LADDER OF ABSTRACTION

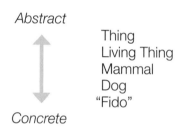

Abstract

Thing
Living Thing
Mammal
Dog
"Fido"

Concrete

Abstraction is, so to speak, the process of leaving out detail.[1] As we move up the ladder from below, our terms become less specific. For example, *Fido* names a category of one; he is a particular brown and white cocker spaniel. But as we move up to the category *dog*, all of Fido's unique characteristics are left behind as we focus only on those features he shares with other dogs. At the next higher level of abstraction, *mammal*, even Fido's "dog-ness" is left behind as we focus on only those features he shares with other mammals (as against, say, fish or trees). And so on, all the way up the ladder of abstraction. The higher we go, the broader, less detailed, and more inclusive our terms become; the lower we move, the more concrete and specific. That's why we can say the process of abstracting (moving up the ladder) is the process of leaving out detail. Korzybski wanted us to understand this process so that we could appreciate both the wonders and the pitfalls of abstractions.

There are those, it seems, who delight in disparaging "mere abstractions," as if we could live without them. But the ability to abstract is in a sense the genius of the human mind. Alligators or mosquitoes or dogs cannot think of abstractions such as *mammals*, or *love*, or *justice*, much less an equation such as $E=MC^2$. They experience the concrete particulars of the world, but they cannot reflect upon them and analyze them. Only humans can create the required abstractions and then put them to use.

"Great thoughts are always general," said Samuel Johnson in his *Lives of the English Poets*. And so they are. Every wise proverb is useful precisely because it represents a powerful abstraction, often in humble dress. Jesus's language was full of the highest-order metaphors (e.g., "I am the way, and the truth, and the life" [John 14:6]), each one embodying a powerful abstraction. The greatest human minds throughout history have been those marked by their ability to think at levels of abstraction that leave most of us behind.

Thus it makes no sense to valorize the concrete at the expense of the abstract. To do so is to induce upon ourselves what C. S. Lewis called a "doglike mind."

> You will have noticed that most dogs cannot understand *pointing*. You point to a bit of food on the floor; the dog, instead of looking at the floor, sniffs at your finger. A finger is a finger to him, and that is all. His world is all fact and no meaning.[2]

A contempt for abstractions consigns us to this doglike mind wherein everything is experienced as an animal experiences it: merely at the level of the particular. But such contempt is misguided. Not only is it a denial of something wonderfully and uniquely human; we could not live without abstractions if we wanted to. Those who complain about abstractions use abstractions (such as the term *abstractions*) to do so. Abstractions are a form of shorthand we cannot do without. They help us manage the complexity of the world around us. They are what make the best of human thought and conversation possible. They are simply indispensable.

DEAD-LEVEL ABSTRACTING

What we should avoid, on the other hand—and what, I suspect, most critics really have in mind when they mistakenly disparage abstractions in general—is what Wendell Johnson called "dead-level abstracting."[3] Hayakawa described this common problem this way: "Some people, it appears, remain more or less permanently stuck at certain levels of the abstraction ladder, some on the lower levels, some on the very high levels." He then quotes Johnson as follows:

> Probably all of us know certain people who seem able to talk on and on without ever drawing any very general conclusions. For example, there is the back-fence chatter that is made up of he said then I said and then she said and I said and then he said, far into the afternoon, ending with, "Well, that's *just* what I told him!" Letters describing vacation trips frequently illustrate this sort of language, detailing places seen, times of arrival and departure, the foods eaten and the prices paid, whether the beds were hard or soft, etc.[4]

Such dead-level conversations on the lower rungs of the ladder can be tiresome and boring. But, at the opposite extreme, others seem equally locked in at the upper levels. Everything remains in the realm of the general, never descending to the particular—what Wendell Johnson calls "words cut loose from their moorings."[5] We have all heard preachers and teachers who fall into this trap, and we have all read dull, obtuse books in which scarcely a concrete statement can be found. This tendency too is to be avoided.

The ability and willingness to move up and down the abstraction ladder is the mark not only of interesting communicators but of clear and sound thinkers as well. The field of general semantics was developed as a way to encourage this kind of good mental hygiene. Effective thinkers/communicators are constantly reflecting on the particulars in such a way as to build useful generalizations and then testing those generalizations again against the particulars. They move up and down the ladder of abstraction, allowing the general to inform and give meaning to the particulars, while allowing the particulars to flesh out and anchor the general.

> No story has power, nor will it last, unless we feel in ourselves that it is true and true of us.
>
> —"Lee," in *East of Eden*

Scientists, for example, build broad hypotheses on the basis of their observations of the details and then design experiments with the details to test their broad hypotheses. Great literature is timeless precisely because it conveys large ideas through the telling of concrete stories. (As someone has said, "Newspapers tell us what *happened*; literature tells us what *happens*.") Great orators and essayists range up and down the ladder in their works, allowing the abstract to provide meaning and context to the particulars, and the particulars to flesh out and bring to life the abstract. Effective preachers and politicians do the same. Says Hayakawa,

> The interesting writer, the informative speaker, the accurate thinker . . . operate on all levels of the abstraction ladder, moving quickly and gracefully and in orderly fashion from the higher to the lower, from lower to higher, with minds as lithe and deft and beautiful as monkeys in a tree.[6]

MAPS AND TERRAIN

Korzybski wanted us to think of our language, filled as it is with abstractions, the way we think of maps. It's a useful metaphor.

Imagine yourself looking for the courthouse in an unfamiliar town. You are parked on a street with a city map open on your lap. From where you sit, you can see through the windshield an almost infinite variety of detail that is not represented on the map: a stop sign, parking meters lining the curb, the high-rise apartments down the block, the hardware store with the bright sign, a large pothole that needs to be fixed, the slope of the pavement down to the next cross street, etc. None of these details show up on the map. The street on which you are parked is reduced there to nothing more than a thin blue line labeled with its name. This in turn is connected to a matrix of other blue lines, each of which is also labeled. Higher up and over to the left on the map you can see a small symbol of a building labeled "Courthouse." It's located there beside its own labeled blue line.

That courthouse is your destination. But to find it you do not need to know about the colorful sign on the hardware store, or the pothole, or the sloping street. Those are details of the terrain that have been "left behind" in this high level abstraction called a "map." For your purposes you need to know only where the courthouse is in relation to where you are and what streets you must take to get there. The infinite variety of the terrain itself has thus been reduced on the paper spread across your knees to a matrix of thin blue lines and assorted symbols, the essential information you need to get you from "here" to "there." This reduced (abstracted) information is all you require. Here, then, are four obvious but important observations about your map:

- First, the map is not the terrain itself. No one would think of confusing the two. We must drive on the streets, not the map.

- Second, the map is merely a high-level abstract representation of the streets. Of necessity it can represent only selected (relevant) details of the actual terrain.

- Third, such an abstraction (map) can be extremely useful, as anyone who has tried to navigate around a strange city without one can testify.

- But, fourth—and this is crucial—such a map is useful only if it accurately corresponds to the terrain it supposedly represents.

The field of general semantics reminds us that our language, and the categories (abstractions) it provides us for our thinking, is like that map. It is our mental representation of the world in which we live. It is not that world itself; it's our abstract map of that world. But as such it is the mental picture that becomes the basis for how we live and act and make our way.

Most people have probably never heard of the abstraction ladder, but they nonetheless move up and down its rungs all day, every day, in what they say and do. Consider, for instance, how many different ways we use, in one form or another, the general-to-specific range suggested by[7] the abstraction ladder: abstract-concrete; theory-practice; hypothesis-facts; principle-application; conceptual-operational; idea-action; universal-individual; the one–the many; thought-behavior; truth-experience; proposition-story; statement-image. We think and act up and down the ladder constantly in the everyday affairs of life, large and small.

DO ABSTRACTIONS MATTER?

A generation ago, University of Chicago professor Richard Weaver published a widely read book entitled *Ideas Have Consequences*.[8] It was an apt title, because how we operate on the upper rungs of the abstraction ladder (our ideas, how we think) affects what takes place toward the bottom of the ladder (how we speak and act). That's why it's so important that we get our maps right.

Consider, for example, the terms of the abortion debate.

At the concrete level (living cells) the two sides of the debate show little disagreement; neither quibbles much with what science can tell us is there. But as we move up the ladder, the corresponding abstractions diverge.

Abstract

Refuse	Human being
Foreign entity	Unborn child
Living cells	Living cells

Concrete

Those who favor keeping abortion legal climb the ladder on the left. The embryo or fetus in the mother's body is, if she says it is, an invasive foreign entity with little moral or civil status of its own. It can be disposed of pretty much at will. Those who oppose legalized abortion, by contrast, climb the ladder on the right. They view that same embryo or fetus as an unborn person whose moral and civil rights must be protected by society. Do such differences matter? They are, after all, "mere abstractions." Yet what could matter more? The abstractions we choose in this debate mean the difference between life and death for millions of unborn children.

Ideas have consequences, very often profound consequences. How we think, our mental map of the world, determines how we speak and act, in this instance as in many others, with the gravest of results.

TWO PROBLEMS

All of the above should alert us to at least two potential problems with our use of language; that is, with our mental maps.

First, *false mental maps let us down.* Working with an inadequate set of categories (abstractions) is like trying to navigate through a complex urban setting with a street map that jumbles the streets, labels them randomly, and locates the courthouse in the wrong place. How likely is it that we would find our destination? In the same way, trying to navigate complex issues with jumbled language and categories is a prescription for confusion. Often the stakes in such confusion are fairly minor: we misunderstand something or unwittingly misrepresent it to others. Being limited, fallible creatures, we do this all the time. But what if the terrain we are seeking to navigate has to do with Christ's purposes for his church? It's essential that we get such an important map right.

This point highlights the purpose of this book. The "word versus deed" debate has been plagued by a variety of inadequate verbal maps. The talk about "preaching the gospel with our deeds" is a classic example. It's a misleading way of thinking (and therefore talking) which in turn has distorting effects as we move down the ladder toward concrete behavior.

The purpose of this book is to lay out a more accurate map of what the Bible actually teaches on this subject. Our goal is to conform our "map" to the Bible's "map"; to shape our categories to the Bible's categories; to fit our way of speaking about this subject to the Bible's way of speaking about it so as to fit our way of behaving to the Bible's instruction. Which of our abstractions, common though they may be, may actually be confusing us instead of helping? What language do we require instead to grasp the Bible's teaching more accurately and then live it out more faithfully? These are the questions this book is attempting to answer.

But this leads to a second potential problem: *What if we're not very good at map reading?* Maps are by definition high-level abstractions. What if, crucial as it may be, abstract thinking is not one of our strengths? This question is not merely hypothetical.

The famous Swiss psychologist Jean Piaget set out a theory of personality development that portrayed children as incapable of abstract thought until well along in their maturing process. According to Piaget, the typical child goes through a pre-operational stage (ages 2 to 7) marked by the acquisition of motor skills and an absence of logical thinking; a concrete operational stage (ages 7 to 12) marked by mostly concrete thinking; and a formal operational stage (age 12 and beyond) where the child finally develops a capacity for abstract logical reasoning.

So far, so good, we may say. Even if we're unwilling to accept Piaget's analysis as the final word, all who have raised children have witnessed some such developmental process at work. But Piaget also made this startling observation: only about 20 percent of the population ever make it past the concrete operational stage. According to Piaget, 80 percent remain, if not incapable of, at least resistant to and not very competent with, significant abstract thought. Some later psychologists suggested that Piaget was too generous; as few as 10 percent of the population, they claimed, are competent in abstract thinking. The rest live out their lives for the most part on the lower rungs of the abstraction ladder.

We need not quibble over percentages. Who really knows? But whatever the percentage, the point is sobering. If good mental hygiene requires us to move freely up and down the abstraction ladder, keeping our abstractions in touch with the concrete levels of life and vice versa, what does that say about those who are not very good at abstract thinking? The higher the abstraction, the more they tune out. If most people are less than competent at this level, that bears some large implications, not least for those reading this book.

The purpose of laying out the abstraction ladder in this chapter is to provide us a framework for thinking about the relationship between *word* (more abstract) and *deed* (more concrete) in the calling of the church. What's more, the abstraction ladder itself is a high level abstraction, as are such concepts as *verbal* and *nonverbal* communication. These are useful categories designed to help us "map the terrain" of our present discussion, but the metaphor of mapping the terrain is itself a high-level abstraction. Our entire discussion is awash in valuable but high-order abstractions. Thus the very reading of this book assumes a certain competence in abstract, theoretical thinking. Is this a task only a small percentage of the population can manage?

I confess that I do not know the answer to that question. But I do know this: while all of us must live and operate at the concrete level, abstract thinking is also a crucially important skill. As Hayakawa reminds us, effective thinkers and communicators operate on all levels of the abstraction ladder. In our "word versus deed" discussion we need thinkers who will not shy away from the world of abstractions, precisely because these abstractions, as we shall see in the following chapters, have such a shaping influence on our actual practice.

CHAPTER 5

THEOLOGY APPLIED

The faithful do not only make claims with their lips, but prove their service of God in concrete acts.

—John Calvin

We have said that while the gospel can only be preached verbally, there is undeniably also a nonverbal dimension to our gospel obligations. God calls his people to demonstrate the gospel at the concrete levels of life; that is, in the way we live. The mission of Christ's church is thus both word *and* deed. Those deeds may not be able to *proclaim* the gospel, but they are the primary means by which we *enact* the gospel before a watching world. With the previous chapter's discussion in hand we are now in a position to explore this nonverbal dimension of our calling.

THE NATURE OF THE BIBLE

All of the Bible can be arrayed, so to speak, up and down the ladder of abstraction. The substance of the Bible's message is theology (abstract) applied to life (concrete). There is not much in the Scriptures that cannot be located somewhere on this continuum.

It's important to recognize that the Bible is not first and foremost about us. The Bible is *theocentric* (God-centered), not *anthropocentric* (us-centered). It is first about God's person, his nature, his ways, his actions, his will, his design, his purposes, his view of things—and only secondarily and derivatively about us and what our response to him should be. It is in this sense that we can say that the Bible is "theology applied." *This is what is true of him*, the Bible keeps telling us, in one form or another, *and so this is what should be true of us.*

Consider the apostle Paul's reference to "oxen" in his appeal to the Corinthians:

> Who serves as a soldier at his own expense? Who plants a vineyard without eating any of its fruit? Or who tends a flock without getting some of the milk? Do I say these things on human authority? Does not the Law say the same? For it is written in the Law of Moses, "You shall not muzzle an ox when it treads out the grain." Is it for oxen that God is concerned? Does he not certainly speak for our sake? It was written for our sake, because the plowman should plow in hope and the thresher thresh in hope of sharing in the crop. If we have sown spiritual things among you, is it too much if we reap material things from you? (1 Cor. 9:7–11)

The concrete application to oxen in Deuteronomy 25 was the outworking, Paul says, of a broader, more abstract principle that included not only work animals but soldiers, vine dressers, shepherds, plowmen, threshers, and Christian workers. It is essentially the same principle Jesus applied to his disciples when he sent them out two by two: "The laborer deserves his wages" (Luke 10:7). This abstract principle reflects an important element of justice in God's design for

[Jesus's] words and deeds belonged to each other, the words interpreting the deeds and the deeds embodying the words. He did not only announce the good news of the kingdom; he performed visible "signs of the kingdom."
—John Stott

human society. It is this broader insight, Paul says, that is at work in the law's concrete reference to oxen, on the one hand, and speaks to his own situation in Corinth, on the other. Paul's entire argument is arrayed up and down the ladder of abstraction.

The stories of the Bible are another case in point. They do not merely report the details of what happened. They do that well enough, but if that's all we receive from them, we will have missed their primary intent. The Bible's stories are recounted for a reason. They are not usually there to supply us broad moralistic examples; they are designed to show us what we need to know of God—his person, his nature, his ways, his actions, his will, his design, his plan, his purposes, his view of things—and then through that, in the end, what we need to know about ourselves and our responses. And these theological insights are typically well up the ladder from the concrete details of the stories themselves (see 1 Cor. 10:1–13).

The opposite is also true. The high-order abstract truths in the Bible (e.g., "God is holy," Ps. 99:9) are not designed to be retained in the abstract. They bear with them "entailments."[1] Their implications are to be worked out in the details of our lives ("Be holy, for I am holy," Lev. 11:44–45; 1 Pet. 1:16). The broad promises of the Bible ("I will never leave you nor forsake you," Heb. 13:5) are to be trusted and acted upon. God's general commands ("Love your neighbor as yourself," e.g., Lev. 19:18; Matt. 19:19) are intended to be lived out in the detail of our daily existence. All of the Bible is arrayed up and down the ladder of abstraction.

This is why we can say that the Bible is "theology applied." Not every passage explicitly exhibits the ladder's full range, but some such range is implicit everywhere. The details can only be made sense of in light of the larger, more abstract truths, while those abstract truths always bear implications for the details of our lives. The Bible is constantly, either explicitly or implicitly, dealing with the relationship between the two.

TRUTH AND ITS CONSEQUENCES

What are the consequences of deciding
the following generalization is true?

General   If: *There is no such thing as resur-*
rection of the dead.

Then: *Christ has not been raised.*
Your faith is futile.
You are still in your sins.
Those who have died in Christ are lost.
I am a liar.
Specific   *We are of all people most to be pitied.*

1 Cor. 15:12–20

None of this should surprise us. God designed us to live on this ladder. We are embodied persons making our way in the physical and social world God has made; all of us experience a variety of concrete needs and inclinations. But we are also thinking, feeling, spiritual creatures. We are made in God's image and share aspects of his nature. Unlike the lesser creatures, we crave the meaning, significance, and purpose that only the larger truths can provide. We live our lives on the abstraction ladder, from top to bottom.

Alfred Korzybski was right. The healthiest people are those who can range nimbly up and down this ladder, allowing the more general truths to shape and inform the specifics of their lives, even while requiring and embracing those specifics as a way of anchoring, enlivening, and enacting the general. The Bible is designed to instruct us in every part of this process, from large to small.

Some entire books of the Bible reflect this pattern. For instance, the six chapters of Ephesians divide elegantly into two halves. The first three explore in broad strokes what God is doing in the world through Christ. Such ideas are necessarily high and large and abstract. God's purpose, he says, was:

> To bring to light for everyone what is the plan of the mystery hidden for ages in God who created all things, so that through the church the manifold wisdom of God might now be made known to the rulers and authorities in the heavenly places. This was according to the eternal purpose that he has realized in Christ Jesus our Lord. (3:9–11)

The next three chapters, however, deal with the equally concrete details of life. They include such specific instructions as these:

> Sexual immorality and all impurity or covetousness must not even be named among you, as is proper among saints. Let there be no filthiness nor foolish talk nor crude joking, which are out of place, but instead let there be thanksgiving. (5:3–4)

How are the two halves of Ephesians, the abstract and the concrete, related? The bridge is found in 4:1: "I . . . urge you to walk in a manner worthy of the calling to which you have been called." The abstract truths of chapters 1–3 constitute the "calling" of the church, a calling which bears concrete implications for how God's people are to live. Our behavior receives its shape and meaning from the abstract truths of which it is an expression. Neither can stand

> Let us not love in word or talk but in deed and in truth.
> —1 John 3:18

alone: *Truth-informed behavior* and *behavior-enacted truth* are two sides of the same coin.

The large ideas of God's Word, then, always bear implications for how we are to live. Sometimes those ideas are
1. focused on *who God is*: "Anyone who does not love does not know God, because God is love" (1 John 4:8). Or they
2. focus on *what God has done*: "Therefore, brothers, since we have confidence to enter the holy places by the blood of Jesus, by the new and living way that he opened for us through the curtain, that is, through his flesh, and since we have a great priest over the house of God, let us. . . . Let us. . . . Let us . . . " (Heb. 10:19–25). Or perhaps they tell
3. us about *what God will yet do*: "The day of the Lord will come like a thief, and then the heavens will pass away with a roar, and the heavenly bodies will be burned up and dissolved, and the earth and the works that are done on it will be exposed. Since all these things are thus to be dissolved, what sort of people ought you to be in lives of holiness and godliness?" (2 Pet. 3:10–11).

One way or another, God's truth always bears implications for our living. Hence Paul's prayer that the Colossians might "be filled with the knowledge of his will in all spiritual wisdom and understanding." Why? "So as to walk in a manner worthy of the Lord, fully pleasing to him, bearing fruit in every good work" (Col. 1:9–10). There it is in a nutshell— *theology applied.*

FAITH AND WORKS

So strong is the connection between the general and the specific, abstract truth and its concrete expression, in the Christian life that defaulting on either may call into question the whole. The all-encompassing abstract proposition, "Jesus is Lord," for example, is the very hallmark of the believer. No one can sincerely affirm it, says the apostle Paul, except by the

Holy Spirit (1 Cor. 12:3). In fact, the failure to do so is the surest sign of a lack of genuineness (2 John 7–11), whatever our behavior. But the opposite is also true. The book of James famously connects the abstract with the concrete in its discussion of faith and works: "What good is it, my brothers, if someone says he has faith but does not have works? Can that faith save him?" (2:14).

What does James mean here by "that faith," the kind that cannot save? It is the faith, he says, of the demons: "You believe that God is one; you do well. Even the demons believe—and shudder!" (v. 19). The faith that cannot save is a faith that perches high up the ladder and never comes down. It consists of little more than mental assent to Israel's ancient *Sh'ma*: "The LORD our God, the LORD is one" (Deut. 6:4). But this minimalist monotheistic acknowledgement, understood all too well in the demonic realm, is not a faith that saves. The faith that saves takes in the next verse in Deuteronomy as well: "You shall love the LORD your God with all your heart and with all your soul and with all your might" (v. 5).[2] While genuine saving faith certainly includes elements of mental assent, it also includes more. It involves personally entrusting ourselves to God and obeying his Word in gospel-worthy deeds—something the demons will never do.

Note that this kind of faith, the faith that saves, does not disdain or repudiate the abstract. On the contrary, it stands in full agreement with the demons on the great abstract affirmation of the *Sh'ma*: *our God is one*. Genuine faith, in fact, hungers for *more* abstract knowledge about God. Who is he? What are his attributes? What is he like? What are his ways? The difference is that saving faith does not *settle* for the abstract. It wants to know not only *about* God; it seeks to know him personally and to serve him faithfully. It wants to honor him and worship him and fellowship with him. It seeks to understand his will and obey it. It aspires to live a life "worthy of his calling" (2 Thess. 1:11) in every possible way. This is what distinguishes biblical faith from mere mental assent. The real thing is lived all up and down the ladder of abstraction. Anything short of this, the Bible warns, may not be genuine faith at all.

CHAPTER SIX

GOSPEL-WORTHY DEEDS

> Christians cannot be governed by mere principles. Principles [can] carry one only so far. At some point every person must . . . know what God [is] calling him to do.
>
> —Eric Metaxas, *Bonhoeffer*

All we have said so far, then, is why we must not choose between the verbal and nonverbal dimensions of God's calling. The gospel that can only be communicated by putting it into words inevitably bears implications for our behavior. It is a gospel that not only must be preached; it must be lived. It must be *incarnated* in the concrete details of our lives, *enacted* by Christ's church before a watching world.[1] All of our behavior is to be shaped and informed by that gospel. "Whatever happens," says the apostle Paul, "conduct yourselves in a manner worthy of the gospel of Christ" (Phil. 1:27 NIV; see also 1 Thess. 2:12).

What does such gospel-worthy conduct look like? According to the Bible, gospel-worthy conduct is lived out in five distinguishable circles of application: personal life, family, God's people, society at large, and the natural world. We may think of them as concentric circles of our service to God, with the issues of our personal allegiance to him at the center.

1) PERSONAL LIFE

Contemporary discussions of gospel-worthy conduct often veer immediately to the social demands of the gospel, either taking for granted or ignoring altogether the private dimensions of the Christian life. The reasons for this, I suspect, are at least threefold.

First, our time and place in history is stamped with the radical individualism of the Enlightenment. In reacting against this imbalance some may be inclined to move directly, and perhaps too quickly, to the social and corporate implications of the gospel, bypassing the individual realm entirely. Second, in certain Christian circles the personal dimensions of Christian living—issues of sexual morality, personal honesty, worldliness, etc.—seem to be as far as the demands of the gospel ever reach. These issues are stressed constantly, but little is heard of the social implications of the gospel. Such a perceived imbalance undoubtedly prompts others to leapfrog these "overworked" private matters on their way to broader social concerns. Third, any emphasis on issues of personal holiness in the Christian life appears for some to be an embarrassment. They tend to write off such concerns as the unwarranted obsession of pietists.

Yet whatever the reasons—some more worthy than others—it is potentially a serious mistake to allow any or all of them to blind us to the clear teaching of the Bible. The private issues of the heart come first with God. Not only is religious practice empty without the right interior orientation (Luke 18:9–14); so also is our social action: "If I give all I possess to the poor . . . but have not love, I gain nothing" (1 Cor. 13:3 NIV). Our social obligations rank high with the Lord, but if we are to fulfill them aright they must be the outworking of our preeminent obligation, which is to love, worship, and serve God with all our hearts (see Matt. 10:37; Luke 14:26). Moving too quickly to our social obligations can blind us to this reality, leading to external behavior as hollow and sterile as that of the Pharisees.

"If you love me," Jesus said, "you will keep my commandments" (John 14:15). We hear Jesus's commands throughout both his teaching and that of his apostles. Time and again these commands focus on both the condition of our hearts and the details of our private lives: how we pray, what we do with our money, the purity of our sexual lives, our integrity, our personal godliness, and so on. Our private lives are where the business of gospel-worthy conduct begins.

2) FAMILY

The second circle of application is our family. God's truth entails specific obligations to those closest to us.

> The family relationships into which we are born imply the lasting commitment of the family's members to one another. . . . It is part of being human.
>
> —John Goldingay

The Christian's one and only allegiance is to Jesus Christ. He alone is Lord and our loyalty to him transcends all others (Luke 14:26). Yet he is the very one who instructs us about our God-given familial responsibilities. Our several obligations to our family are thus *derived from* our single and ultimate commitment to him. It is he who calls us to be faithful mothers, fathers, husbands, wives, and children and who provides in his Word a body of instruction in how to do so.

This biblical teaching spans the Old and New Testaments. At times it is couched in the abstract: "Honor your father and your mother, as the LORD your God commanded you" (Deut. 5:16). At other times it is very concrete indeed: "The husband should give to his wife her conjugal rights, and likewise the wife to her husband" (1 Cor. 7:3). But at whatever level they are found, our family obligations are not to be avoided. According to the Bible, "If anyone does not provide for his relatives, and especially for members of his household, he has denied the faith and is worse than an unbeliever" (1 Tim. 5:8).

Significantly, this was a priority Jesus himself modeled. In the moment of his supreme anguish he demonstrated the principle that our first circle of *social* obligation pertains to those closest to us:

> Standing by the cross of Jesus were his mother and his mother's sister. . . . When Jesus saw his mother and the disciple whom he loved standing nearby, he said to his mother, "Woman, behold, your son!" Then he said to the disciple, "Behold, your mother!" And from that hour the disciple took her to his own home. (John 19:25–27)

3) GOD'S PEOPLE

The third and next largest circle of application is God's people (1 Pet. 2:10). The vast majority of the Bible's instructions concerning the believer's social obligations are focused here.

This may be surprising to many. They have become so accustomed to hearing biblical passages wrenched from this context and applied to society at large that they have come to take such a move for granted. But this sort of decontextualizing, though common, represents a serious distortion of the Scriptures. We will explore this mistake more fully later, but for the present we must settle for this observation: when the Bible calls us to a concern for others, it is most often speaking of our obligations to our brothers and sisters within the believing community.

Why is this point so often ignored? In their eagerness to demonstrate God's concern for—and to remedy the church's relative negligence toward—society's disadvantaged, advocates sometimes handle the Scriptures rather carelessly. Some may believe their worthy ends justify the means. Others may simply be oblivious to the problem. But whatever the reason, they appear untroubled about using biblical passages in a way that fails their context.

Biblical Bright Lines. Some seem to have a different problem: they are uncomfortable with the exclusivism inherent in drawing too bright a line between the believing community and society at large. They do not wish to privilege the one over the other. We have obligations to both, they will argue; the boundaries between the two need not be emphasized.

> For you are a people holy to the LORD your God, and the LORD has chosen you to be a people for his treasured possession, out of all the peoples who are on the face of the earth.
> —Deut. 14:2

The problem with this line of thinking is that the Bible stresses the opposite. In the Old Testament, for example, the boundaries between those within and without the community of God's people could not have been drawn more brightly. Almost every aspect of the Mosaic Law was designed to distinguish Israel from the other peoples. Attempts to blur this distinction (such as intermarriage[2]) were strictly forbidden. "You shall be holy to me," Israel was instructed, "for I the LORD am holy and have separated you from the peoples" (Lev. 20:26; see also Deut. 14:2; 26:16–19).

In the New Testament the boundaries are drawn with equal clarity. God's people are instructed to keep these lines very bright indeed:

> Do not be unequally yoked with unbelievers. For what partnership has righteousness with lawlessness? Or what fellowship has light with darkness? What accord has Christ with Belial? Or what portion does a believer share with an unbeliever? What agreement has the temple of God with idols? For we are the temple of the living God. (2 Cor. 6:14–16)

Jesus said, "Whoever is not with me is against me, and whoever does not gather with me scatters" (Matt. 12:30). If we are embarrassed by these sorts of bright-line distinctions between God's people and those outside the believing community, our problem is with the Bible. The Scriptures maintain these boundaries across the Testaments.

> Do you not know that the saints will judge the world?
> —1 Cor. 6:2

This is why losing sight of them can quickly lead to a mishandling of the biblical text. We do not have the right to assume that what pertains to the one community automatically pertains (much less pertains in the same way) to the other. Yet this is what happens when advocates extract from their context passages directed to life within the community of God's people and apply them directly to life beyond that community. It's a prescription for misusing the Bible.

Social Action Passages. The difficulty for those who want to emphasize our social obligations to the world at large is, as noted above, that most of the "social action" passages of the Bible are not addressed to that broader context. With the significant exceptions of Proverbs and the book of Job (see chapter 7), the Old Testament typically focuses Israel's social obligations in-house. The relevant passages in the Psalms, for example, assume a theocratic context, a point emphasized by the many references to "God's people" throughout the Psalter. As for the law,[3] Deuteronomy 15 is typical:

> At the end of every seven years you must cancel debts. This is how it is to be done: Every creditor shall cancel the loan he has made to his *fellow Israelite*. He shall not require payment from his *fellow Israelite or brother*, because the LORD's time for canceling debts has been proclaimed. You may require payment from a *foreigner*, but you must cancel any debt your *brother* owes you. . . . If there is a poor man among *your brothers* in any of the towns of the land that the LORD

your God is giving you, do not be hardhearted or tightfisted toward your poor *brother*. Rather be openhanded and freely lend him whatever he needs. . . . Give generously to him and do so without a grudging heart. . . . There will always be poor people in the land. Therefore I command you to be openhanded toward your *brothers* and toward the poor and needy in your land. If a *fellow Hebrew, a man or a woman*, sells himself to you and serves you six years, in the seventh year you must let him go free. And when you release him, do not send him away empty-handed. Supply him liberally from your flock, your threshing floor and your winepress. (Deut. 15:1–14 NIV)

Instructions about caring for the poor in the New Testament are equally focused on the believer's obligations to fellow believers. From the beginning (Acts 4:32–35; 6:1–2) Christians were called to care for the needs of their fellow Christians. Passage after passage in the New Testament reflects this emphasis.[4] In fact, this was James's concern in his widely cited passage on faith and works:

If a *brother or sister* is poorly clothed and lacking in daily food, and one of you says to them, "Go in peace, be warmed and filled," without giving them the things needed for the body, what good is that? So also faith by itself, if it does not have works, is dead. (James 2:15–17; see also 2:2)

We will never effectively demonstrate Christ's love to the world, if we cannot first demonstrate it to the Church—the *whole* Church, and that includes those struggling just to survive.
—Richard Stearns

After our families, the social implications of the gospel focus first and foremost on fellow members of the body of Christ. This is no doubt due to the unique spiritual relationship each Christian shares with Jesus himself, and therefore with one another. As Paul says to the Corinthians, Christ's body "does not consist of one member but of many. . . . If one member suffers, all suffer together; if one member is honored, all rejoice together. Now you are the body of Christ and individually members of it" (1 Cor. 12:14, 26–27).

4) SOCIETY AT LARGE

In his classic statement of the Christian's broader social obligations, the apostle Paul wrote to the Galatians: "So then, as we have opportunity, let us do good to everyone, and especially to those who are of the household of faith" (Gal. 6:10). Here we see reflected, first, the Christian's primary obligation (*malista*, "most of all," "especially") to fellow members of Christ's body; but also, second, our broader obligations to all people.

The Biblical Focus. It is just here, however, that if we are to do justice to the Bible we must face honestly the point made in the previous section. The Bible does not itself spend much time exploring in any explicit way the believer's obligations in this fourth realm. The Scriptures speak often in the abstract of God's concern for mercy, justice, and love in human affairs, and it regularly moves down the ladder of abstraction with a variety of specific applications of this truth within both the family and the community of believers. But there is surprisingly little in the Bible that addresses, in equally concrete terms, how believers are to live out these priorities beyond the believing community.

In the Law and Prophets, for instance, the closest we come are those passages dealing with Israel's obligations to "aliens," "foreigners," or "sojourners." But even these instructions related to non-Israelites who were resident within or passing through Israel's boundaries. These instructions were thus about how to treat visitors and outsiders fairly and hospitably within God's theocratic community. They had little to say in any direct way about the Israelite's social obligations beyond those borders. There is nothing explicit in the Old Testament to suggest, for example, that Israelites were to pursue an agenda of social justice amidst the surrounding peoples or the broader Gentile world.

Similarly, New Testament instructions focus heavily on life within the church. They are much concerned with issues of equity and compassion there, but they have correspondingly little to say about the external, secular community. The Old Testament's focus on social issues within the covenant community's boundaries—that is, God's intent for his people's relationships with one another and their success or failure in fulfilling that intent—is clearly evident in the New Testament; it shows itself in a variety of passages dealing with the believer's social obligations to other believers. But there are relatively few passages that focus similar obligations beyond "the household of faith." We are obliged to do good to *all people*, Paul informs us, but what does this general instruction mean in practice? Neither Jesus, nor Paul, nor the other New Testament writers spell it out.

Jesus and the Gentiles. During his earthly life Jesus actually had little to do with the world beyond the believing community. The most he had to say about the social world beyond Israel (in his case, Rome) were statements such as, "Render to Caesar the things that are Caesar's" (Mark 12:17). On the few occasions when he

> Do not give dogs what is holy, and do not throw your pearls before pigs, lest they trample them underfoot and turn to attack you.
>
> —Matt. 7:6

made contact with that outside world, or it made contact with him, he expended little effort in trying to reform it. Recall, for example, this encounter during his single brief venture beyond Israel's borders into Phoenicia:

> A Canaanite woman . . . came out and was crying, "Have mercy on me, O Lord, Son of David; my daughter is severely oppressed by a demon." But he did not answer her a word. And his disciples came and begged him, saying, "Send her away, for she is crying out after us." He answered, "I was sent only to the lost sheep of the house of Israel." But she came and knelt before him, saying, "Lord, help me." And he answered, "It is not right to take the children's bread and throw it to the dogs." She said, "Yes, Lord, yet even the dogs eat the crumbs that fall from their masters' table." Then Jesus answered her, "O woman, great is your faith! Be it done for you as you desire." And her daughter was healed instantly. (Matt. 15:22–28)

Jesus neither spoke of nor carried out anything that could be called "social action" in society at large. But, like the Old Testament prophets, he acted decisively and had a great deal to say about conditions *within* the believing community. This was his primary focus. Even his famous Sermon on the Mount focused heavily on brother-to-brother relationships (see Matt. 5:21–24; 7:3–5) and life within the believing community: "And when you pray, do not keep on babbling like pagans, for they think they will be heard because of their many words. Do not be like them, for your Father knows what you need before you ask him" (Matt. 6:7–8 NIV). When the Sermon did turn to external relationships, it was not to lay out an agenda for social action in the surrounding community but to urge love for one's unbelieving persecutors:

> You have heard that it was said, "You shall love your neighbor and hate your enemy." But I say to you, Love your enemies and pray for those who persecute you, so that you may be sons of your Father who is in heaven. For he makes his sun rise on the evil and on the good, and sends rain on the just and on the unjust. For if you love those who love you, what reward do you have? Do not even the tax collectors do the same? And if you greet only your brothers, what more are you doing than others? Do not even the Gentiles do the

same? You therefore must be perfect, as your heavenly Father is perfect. (Matt. 5:43–48)

Jesus was not uninformed or naive about the social injustices beyond Israel's borders—"You know that the rulers of the Gentiles lord it over them, and their great ones exercise authority over them" (Matt. 20:25)—but neither did he address those injustices in any systematic way or seek to remedy them. Nor did his apostles. The New Testament is filled with instructions about our personal lives and our obligations within the family and the church. But beyond a few general instructions about loving and praying for one's enemies, or the apostle's "Let every person be subject to the governing authorities" (Rom. 13:1; see also 1 Pet. 2:13–14), the New Testament is silent on the topic of the believer's social obligations to those outside the church.

An Important Question. How is it, then, that these broader social concerns, concerns about the pressing justice and compassion issues in the world at large, play such a prominent role in our contemporary "word versus deed" discussions? If neither the Old or New Testament offers much by way of instruction about these obligations, does this mean the Bible is silent on the subject? Could the Bible's reticence about these details mean believers bear no such obligations?

Some might appear to think so, given how little attention they devote to them. Their case sometimes sounds something like this: "If God expected his people to spend themselves in social action in society at large or on behalf of

> If our mission is to share the good news, we need to be good news people.
> —Christopher Wright

the natural world (i.e., the environment), we would find in his Word the same sorts of concrete applications for these latter two circles of application that we find for the first three.

The fact that the Scriptures say so little about these two is an indication that fixing society or guarding the environment is not part of the church's mission. The church's calling is to be salt and light in the world by living godly lives and preaching the gospel."

There is, in fact, something to be said for this case. Christians certainly are called to live godly lives and proclaim the gospel. What's more, demonstrating that gospel in our personal lives, families, and the believing community is crucial. On the other hand, we should note that this case is essentially an argument from silence, a notoriously weak form of reasoning.

The Scriptures provide instructive applications in the first three circles, one might respond, but even these are not exhaustive. Here too we must constantly seek out, with the Spirit's help, the gospel's implications for a multitude of contemporary issues the Scriptures do not specifically address. The same is true for our last two circles of application. As we shall see in the following chapters, God has called us to gospel-worthy conduct in all of our relationships. The practical implications of the gospel are arrayed across all five circles of application. If the Bible does not itself spell out these implications—and how could it in a constantly changing world?—under the guidance of his Spirit God expects us to pursue this application ourselves.

> The purpose of the [Abrahamic] covenant was never simply that the creator wanted to have Israel as a special people, irrespective of the fate of the rest of the world. The covenant was there to deal with the sin, and bring about the salvation, of the world.
> —N. T. Wright

The Right Start. Just here, however, is where we must take Paul's admonition to heart: "Do your best to present yourself to God as one approved, a worker who has no need to be ashamed, rightly handling the word of truth" (2 Tim. 2:15). As we move down the ladder from the general truths the Bible clearly teaches to their concrete implications for our contemporary lives, it is crucial that we establish our point of departure rightly and then follow its lead. We must allow the passage to be what it is and say what it says. Otherwise we may find ourselves descending the wrong ladder.

For example, some have attempted to advance a biblical argument for social action in society based on God's ancient promise to Abraham: "Abraham shall surely become a great and mighty nation, and all the nations of the earth shall be blessed in him" (Gen. 18:18). From the beginning, it is argued, God's purposes reached beyond his own people. His intent was to work *through* his people to bless the entire human population, a purpose that is continued in the church today. Our calling is to be a blessing to the world through our deeds of compassion and justice in society at large.

The problem with this line of argument is not its conclusion. God does indeed desire his people to be instruments of justice and compassion in society at large. The problem lies in reducing the Abrahamic blessing to this agenda. According to the Bible, Israel would become a blessing to the nations, as God promised, but it would not be by working a humanitarian social agenda. The blessing was explicitly to come through Abraham's "offspring" (Gen. 22:18; 26:4), a reference to the salvation God would provide the world through Jesus Christ. The apostle Paul made this clear to the Galatians:

> The Scripture, foreseeing that God would justify the Gentiles by faith, preached the gospel beforehand to Abraham, saying, "In you shall all the nations be blessed." So then, those

who are of faith are blessed along with Abraham, the man of faith. (Gal. 3:8–9)

This is the biblical emphasis of the Abrahamic promise. God commissioned both Israel and the church to be a blessing to the world, but the blessing he had in mind centers on their role in mediating the justification (right standing before God) he would make available to all peoples through Abraham's offspring, Jesus Christ. In our handling of this passage, then, we must beware of putting words into God's mouth. We must not shift the focus of the blessing God promised to something else. The Abrahamic blessing to the nations is first and foremost the justification by faith that is now available in Jesus Christ; in other words, it's the gospel Paul promulgated in his own mission to the Gentiles.

It is also true, of course, that when the church is living as "a community of holiness, compassion and justice in a world of sin and suffering,"[5] it will in some broader sense be a beacon of God's kingdom and a harbinger of things to come. In this way too the church may be said to be "a blessing and a light to the nations."[6] But this does not justify the substitution of this follow-on effect for the central emphasis of the promised blessing. The Bible focuses the unspeakable blessing to the nations God promised through Abraham and his descendants (see Rom. 4:16), not on Israel's (or our) deeds of compassion and justice, as important as they are, but on the joyous potential for a right standing before him, available to all, whether Jew or Gentile, who are justified by faith in Jesus Christ. We have no biblical warrant for eclipsing this crucial blessing with a different and lesser one. Let us say it again: we must let the texts of the Bible be what they are and say what they say.

Complicating Issues. We have observed that most of the Bible's concrete applications pertain to our third circle of application, the believing community. Hence, when it comes to society at large we must explore, with the Spirit's guidance, the appropriate applications for ourselves. The problem is, this move down the ladder is often not as simple as it seems.

Virtually all will agree, for example, that the Bible teaches as a general truth that "God loves mercy and justice." The question is, what does this require of *us?* What gospel-worthy conduct follows from such a broad affirmation? One

> We should not under-estimate the difficulty of discerning and following the will of God where justice is concerned.
> —Cornelius Plantinga

response might be as follows: As we move down the ladder from what is true of God to what is to be true of his people at ground level, the Bible provides its own answer. God calls his people to emulate him; that is, because he loves justice and mercy, he calls his people "to do justice, and to love kindness" (Mic. 6:8). But notice that even this instruction remains fairly high on the abstraction ladder. What does it require in actual practice, in the crucible of daily life, to "do justice" and "love kindness"?

Sometimes, of course, the answer to this question is obvious. We see a need; it's a need we can meet; we sense the Spirit's prompting, so we act. The move down the ladder requires little reflection. In the well-worn vernacular of Nike sports, we "just do it." But there are many other occasions where the issues are more ambiguous, and the process is not so simple. In such cases the task of discerning the concrete implications of the gospel can be challenging. How should I as a Christian vote on issues such as immigration policy, or welfare reform, or foreign aid, or AIDS relief? What's the best way to serve this panhandler who is asking me for money? What proportion of our church's time and money should be devoted to church planting versus building homes for the

THE IMPORTANCE OF OUR DEEDS

THE IMPORTANCE OF OUR DEEDS

disadvantaged? Is capital punishment in our society just or unjust? What is my obligation to my desperate neighbor who's about to have an abortion? What's the right balance to strike on the issue of gay rights in our secular society?

> The values embedded in the Bible do not necessarily have a straight-line translation into legislation. For instance, all followers of Jesus are obligated to be concerned for the poor. But that does not mean that they should all be committed to passing a higher minimum wage law. Very bright economists disagree about whether such legislation actually results in helping the poor.
> —John Ortberg

It's one thing to talk about doing justice and mercy in the abstract, but it's often another to know what that means in practice. To alleviate our ambiguity we may be tempted to make the Bible say more than it does, or to translate applications that make sense to us into "Thus saith the Lord" mandates for others. Avoiding these mistakes is important if we are to avoid abusing the Scriptures, not to mention one another.

5) NATURAL CREATION

The fifth circle of application, and the broadest, is that of the natural creation itself. We all exist as part of God's physical world and bear a variety of relations to it. In this realm too, then, there is such a thing as gospel-worthy conduct.

The Bible teaches profound truths about God as the creator and his purposes for the human race within his creation, all of which carry implications for our behavior in the world. Like the previous circle, these implications do not themselves receive detailed attention in the Bible. But we must not take this to mean that there are no such implications or that they can be ignored. It only means that, as above, we are called to work them out for ourselves (see chapter 11).

CONCLUSION

Those who stress the deeds side of the "word versus deed" discussion do not typically focus on the first three circles. Conduct motivated by the gospel is important there too, they may acknowledge, but those realms have long enjoyed the church's attention, not least because the Bible addresses them so fully. What's lacking, they believe, is a clear focus on the fourth and fifth realms. God is calling his people in this generation to rise anew to these pressing concerns, it is said— concerns that include war, poverty, AIDS, hunger, refugees, human trafficking and slavery, economic injustice, immigration, clean air and water, climate change (and its impact on the poor in particular), racism, disease, and political oppression. Gospel-worthy conduct as it relates to these issues is what is so desperately needed, it is said, because these are the "deeds" most lacking in the contemporary church.

Yet, as we have noted, the task of discerning exactly what such issues demand of us is not always simple. It requires us to move from broad claims that God loves mercy and justice, or the abstract principle that we are to do good to all men, or the general premise that we are stewards of God's creation, to the concrete actions required in each instance. Elements of uncertainty and controversy inevitably emerge, complicating the process. And the further we descend from the agreed-upon abstractions, the more evident these complications become. Biases make their appearance. Various (more or less biblical) social and political philosophies—theories of human nature, the law, society, the proper roles of government, private institutions, markets, etc.—begin to manifest themselves. The resulting action agendas inevitably diverge.

Our task here cannot be to sort through these agendas.

The issues are too many and complex. The debates over these agendas continue, and others are better equipped to weigh their merits. But I do want to insist that the effort to develop such agendas is crucial for Christ's church and for each individual Christian. There is an inevitable nonverbal dimension to our calling, one that must work itself out across all five circles of application, including society at large and the natural creation. In these realms, too, Christ calls us to be faithful, not only with our words but with our deeds.

> We affirm that evangelism and sociopolitical involvement are both part of our Christian duty. For both are necessary expressions of our doctrines of God and humankind, our love for our neighbor and our obedience to Jesus Christ.
> —"The Cape Town Commitment," 2010

Some worry that focusing on these latter two realms may make too much of this life and too little of the next; or that stressing these issues leads to a corresponding deemphasis on matters of personal godliness or on the church's verbal witness. These concerns are not groundless; the nineteenth- and twentieth-century versions of the so-called social gospel sometimes exhibited all of these faults. Yet this cannot justify jettisoning the proverbial baby with the bathwater. Social activism may sometimes reflect these unfortunate tendencies, but it need not do so.

The gospel bears profound implications both for this life and the next; for the realm of the personal as well as the social; for both our words and our deeds. Provided our activism genuinely qualifies as gospel-worthy, in the sense that it is truly an enactment of the gospel of Jesus Christ, it will embrace the full range of what God calls his church to be and to do. It will not slight either word or deed.

CHAPTER SEVEN

LIVING WISELY

Because God is self-consistent, what He wills can always be expressed as what wisdom dictates, and the themes of history, law, prophecy and apocalyptic can all be transposed into this key.

—Derek Kidner

We have said that, for the most part, when the Bible spells out the social implications of God's truth, those implications are directed toward the believing community. Yet there are at least five important ways the Bible calls us to social obligations beyond the believing community: godly wisdom, neighbor love, kingdom building, adorning the gospel, and stewardship of the creation. The first of these, godly wisdom, is drawn from the wisdom literature of the Old Testament.

THE BOOK OF PROVERBS

The focus of the Old Testament Law and Prophets is largely the theocratic community of Israel. In one sense we can say the same of the book of Proverbs. Its multiple collections of short sentence-sayings and more extended discourses were designed to facilitate parental instruction (1:8–9) among the Israelites. Its wisdom teachings view the world unwaveringly through the lens of the truth revealed uniquely to Israel, so much so that it can be said that the very starting point of this wisdom is reverence for *Yahweh*, the God of Israel (1:7).

On the other hand, it's also true that Proverbs is devoid

of references to Israel's unique identity, history, and privileges, features such as those summarized by the apostle Paul: "They are Israelites, and to them belong the adoption, the glory, the covenants, the giving of the law, the worship, and the promises. To them belong the patriarchs" (Rom. 9:4–5). These features play a prominent shaping role throughout most of the Old Testament, but not in the book of Proverbs. Its wisdom is couched higher up the ladder of abstraction. It tends to speak not of Israel in particular but of humanity in general. Says Bruce Waltke, "By their nature proverbs express eternal truths applicable to many situations."[1]

This broader orientation sets the Proverbs apart from most of the historical, legal, and prophetic portions of the Old Testament. Thus, when this compilation of wisdom—drawn, in part, even from non-Israelite sources—speaks of God's heart for, or the reader's social obligations to, the poor, its references are broad enough to encompass not only our third circle of application, the believing community, but also our fourth, society at large. Consider, for example, what we learn from these instructions:

> The righteous care about justice for the poor,
>   but the wicked have no such concern. (Prov. 29:7 NIV)

> Whoever oppresses a poor man insults his Maker,
>   but he who is generous to the needy honors him.
>   (Prov. 14:31)

> Whoever gives to the poor will not want,
>   but he who hides his eyes will get many a curse.
>   (Prov. 28:27)

> Whoever despises his neighbor is a sinner,
>   but blessed is he who is generous to the poor.
>   (Prov. 14:21)

A generous man will himself be blessed,
    for he shares his food with the poor.
        (Prov. 22:9 NIV)

Whoever is generous to the poor lends to the LORD,
    and he will repay him for his deed. (Prov. 19:17)

Speak up for those who cannot speak for themselves,
    for the rights of all who are destitute.
Speak up and judge fairly;
    defend the rights of the poor and needy.
        (Prov. 31:8–9 NIV)

The book of Proverbs not only echoes the universal biblical testimony about God's concern for the poor; it supplies us relatively concrete applications of that truth. We are not to mock or show contempt for the poor. Nor are we to shut our eyes to their needs. We must not oppress or exploit them. Instead, when "the fallow ground of the poor would yield much food, but it is swept away through injustice" (13:23), we are to care about justice for the one being ill-treated. We are to speak up for the defenseless and defend their rights. We are to give to the needy and be kind to them, sharing our food with them. Thus does Proverbs spell out some of our concrete obligations to the poor, not only within the believing community but beyond it.

What makes such references unusual in the Old Testament is their broader focus on humanity in general. The Law and the Prophets call Israel to similar actions, stemming from the same theological premises, but there the actions are focused on life within the theocratic community. This context is significant and not to be ignored; it must not be brushed aside as irrelevant. We do not have the right merely to assume that whatever is said of that setting automatically applies, equally and in the same way, beyond it. Perhaps it does; perhaps it doesn't; it's an interpretational case that must be made, not simply assumed. But the book of Proverbs legitimately leapfrogs this issue. Its wisdom is couched in terms broad enough (humanity in general) to transcend the social circles. What it says to us thus speaks of our obligations not only to our fellow believers but also to our fellow human beings.

THE BOOK OF JOB

"In the land of Uz there lived a man whose name was Job." So begins the Old Testament book that bears this man's name (Job 1:1 NIV). Yet no one knows who Job was, when he lived, where Uz was located, who wrote the book, or when it was written. The name of the God of Israel is found throughout the book, but like Proverbs, there is no reference to Israel's unique history or institutions (priesthood, laws, tabernacle, feasts, etc.). The book even shows signs of non-Israelite influences. In this sense, Job is probably the least "Jewish" of all the Old Testament books.

This means that, like Proverbs, the wisdom of Job is couched high on the ladder of abstraction, high enough to subsume both our third and fourth circles of application. Job's very anonymity makes him "everyman," so to speak, and his story is addressed to, and is relevant to, not just God's people but all people. This is especially true when it comes to the book's repeated references to the poor and the vulnerable.

The book of Job requires close attention in its interpretation due to its various speeches and dialogues. Sometimes Job is the speaker, sometimes his wife, sometimes his unreliable friends, and sometimes God. On occasion Job and the others speak wisely and truthfully, at other times foolishly, and in the end God must rebuke them all. But when carefully handled, the book of Job reveals a consistent concern for the poor and oppressed similar to that of Proverbs.

As the book unfolds, of course, it shows Job being stripped of almost everything he cared about in the world. This eventually leads to the confused counsel of his friends and Job's misguided protests about God's unfairness. Yet in the process we learn something of Job's prior life. Says he:

> I delivered the poor who cried for help,
>   and the fatherless who had none to help him.
> The blessing of him who was about to perish came
>   upon me,
>   and I caused the widow's heart to sing for joy.
> I put on righteousness, and it clothed me;
>   my justice was like a robe and a turban.
> I was eyes to the blind
>   and feet to the lame.
> I was a father to the needy,
>   and I searched out the cause of him whom I did not
>   know.
> I broke the fangs of the unrighteous and made him drop his
>   prey
>   from his teeth. (29:12–17)

Job portrays himself as a man who rescued the poor, cared for the orphan, ministered to the dying, and blessed the needy widow. He stood up for what was right and championed justice. He served the blind and the crippled; he protected the foreigner who was being ill-treated; he snatched the victim from the jaws of their wicked oppressors. And apparently Job's self-portrayal was an accurate one. Not only did God not refute Job's description; he reinforced it. God called him, "my servant Job" (1:8; 2:3; 42:7–8). Said the Lord, "There is none like him on the earth, a blameless and upright man, who fears God and turns away from evil" (1:8). Job was a man of whose life God approved. As such he becomes a model for us all.

Here again we discover the Scriptures providing concrete applications that speak directly to the human situation.

THE IMPORTANCE OF OUR DEEDS

They tell us of our obligations not only to our fellow believers but to our fellow human beings. They are the sorts of obligations the apostle Paul had in mind when he exhorted Christ's followers to "do good to everyone" (Gal. 6:10; see also 1 Pet. 2:17).

CHAPTER EIGHT

OBEYING THE KING

> When somebody's hurt, you don't run away from them. You run to them. And these people are hurt bad. . . . There's a definition of sin. And that's not doing what you know is right.
>
> —Participant in a Haiti Missions Project

How does the gospel call us to action beyond the believing community? A second line of argument focuses on the issue of obedience to Christ's command to love our neighbor as ourselves.

LOVING OUR NEIGHBOR

If our Lord's Great Commission —"Go into all the world and proclaim the gospel to the whole creation" (Mark 16:15)— is focused on the church's verbal task, his commandment to "love your neighbor as yourself" (Mark 12:30–31; Luke 10:27; see also Gal. 5:14) is a call to our nonverbal responsibilities. We must not overstate this distinction, for sharing the gospel verbally with our neighbor is also, at its best, a profound act of love. But according to the Scriptures genuine neighbor love involves more than our words. God's people are to love their neighbors with their deeds. This clear commandment constitutes a crucial biblical rationale for our social action in the world at large.

The Baseline. According to the apostle Paul, the baseline

for our neighbor love is a commitment to do no harm: "The commandments, 'You shall not commit adultery, You shall not murder, You shall not steal, You shall not covet,' and any other commandment, are summed up in this word: 'You shall love your neighbor as yourself.' Love does no wrong to a neighbor; therefore love is the fulfilling of the law" (Rom. 13:9–10). Whatever else our love may require, it begins by doing no injury. This is the least we owe our neighbor.

But of course our neighborly obligations do not end there. Genuine neighbor love requires more, as epitomized in Jesus's account of the Good Samaritan.

The Good Samaritan. In an attempt to evade the implications of his own summary of God's law, a summary which included the instruction to "love your neighbor as yourself," a man who should have known better ("an expert in the law" [Luke 10:25 NIV]) posed an evasive, self-serving question to Jesus. "Desiring to justify himself," Luke says, he asked Jesus: "Who is my neighbor?" (v. 29). Jesus responded:

> A man was going down from Jerusalem to Jericho, and he fell among robbers, who stripped him and beat him and departed, leaving him half dead. Now by chance a priest was going down that road, and when he saw him he passed by on the other side. So likewise a Levite, when he came to the place and saw him, passed by on the other side. But a Samaritan, as he journeyed, came to where he was, and when he saw him, he had compassion. He went to him and bound up his wounds, pouring on oil and wine. Then he set him on his own animal and brought him to an inn and took care of him. And the next day he took out two denarii and gave them to the innkeeper, saying, "Take care of him, and whatever more you spend, I will repay you when I come back." (Luke 10:30–35)

"Which of these three," Jesus asked when he finished his story, "proved to be a neighbor to the man who fell among the robbers?" The lawyer answered, "The one who showed him mercy," to which Jesus replied, "You go, and do likewise" (vv. 36–37).

In our eagerness to apply Jesus's teaching to settings beyond the believing community, we must first recognize the strong Jewish, theocratic context of this passage. James 2:8 speaks of "the royal law according to the Scripture, 'You shall love your neighbor

> If we love our neighbor as God made him, we must inevitably be concerned for his total welfare, the good of his soul, his body and his community.
> —John Stott

as yourself.'" The Old Testament reference James cites here is the word Moses was commanded (see Lev. 19:1–2) to speak on God's behalf "to all the congregation of the people of Israel": "Do not hate a *fellow Israelite* in your heart. . . . Do not seek revenge or bear a grudge against anyone *among your people*, but love your neighbor as yourself. I am the LORD" (Lev. 19:17–18 NIV).

In the above account we hear two Israelites discussing the essence of this Jewish requirement. The man who was set upon by robbers was himself apparently also a Jew. This is indicated by his location (Jerusalem to Jericho) and the fact that anything other would have required comment. Moreover, the point of the story demands it. The Old Testament was clear about the obligations Jewish brothers owed one another. Yet in violation of these duties, the victim was left to perish by

> If any of your fellow Israelites become poor and are unable to support themselves among you, help them as you would a foreigner and stranger, so they can continue to live among you.
> —Lev. 25:35 (NIV)

his pious fellow Jews, in contrast to being accorded genuine neighbor love by a despised outsider. This is precisely the contrast that makes the story so powerful.

Yet it is also this contrast which broadens the story's applicability. By valorizing the behavior of the outsider Jesus was demonstrating that this sort of neighbor love is not just for insiders. "By depicting a Samaritan helping a Jew," says Tim Keller, "Jesus could not have found a more forceful way to say that anyone at all in need—regardless of race, politics, class, and religion—is your neighbor."[1] Neighbor love is about brother-to-brother relations, but it also transcends those boundaries. *This is what genuine neighbor love looks like*, Jesus is saying, *whoever may be involved*. It's an ethic that extends beyond the believing community to society at large, even to one's enemies, even to those who are ungrateful and evil:

> But I say to you who hear, Love your enemies, do good to those who hate you, bless those who curse you, pray for those who abuse you. To one who strikes you on the cheek, offer the other also, and from one who takes away your cloak do not withhold your tunic either. Give to everyone who begs from you, and from one who takes away your goods do not demand them back. And as you wish that others would do to you, do so to them. If you love those who love you, what benefit is that to you? For even sinners love those who love them. And if you do good to those who do good to you, what benefit is that to you? For even sinners do the same. And if you lend to those from whom you expect to receive, what credit is that to you? Even sinners lend to sinners, to get back the same amount. But love your enemies, and do good, and lend, expecting nothing in return, and your reward will be great, and you will be sons of the Most High, for he is kind to the ungrateful and the evil. Be merciful, even as your Father is merciful. (Luke 6:27–36; see also Matt. 5:43–45)

DEFINING OUR NEIGHBOR

So, then, what should the lawyer have learned from Jesus's answer to his question? According to this passage, who does Jesus say is our neighbor? How might we summarize his point?

We should note that some will immediately resist any such summary. When asked to define "neighbor," they will say, Jesus did not answer with an abstraction. He responded with a story. We do him a disservice, then, if we try to translate his story into some sort of general proposition.

This all-too-common complaint offers the illusion of being both wise and faithful to Jesus's teaching, but it is neither. To be sure, Jesus couched his answer at the concrete level, low on the ladder of abstraction; he told a story full of vivid detail. But

> A poet should address the specific, and if there be anything about him, he will articulate the universal.
> —Goethe

when he said "Go and do likewise," he was obviously referring to something more universal (abstract) than the specifics of what to do when you find an injured man beside the Jericho road. The details of the story were his indirect way of making a broader, more abstract point about showing mercy in general, a point that has wide applicability.[2] Jesus refrained from providing this abstraction not because he disdained propositions, but for his own widely ignored but clearly stated pedagogical reasons.[3] He regularly required his listeners to do the work of discerning his larger point for themselves: "He who has ears to hear, let him hear" (Matt. 11:15). Thus any refusal to reflect on that larger point not only does not honor Jesus's teaching; it evades it.

So let us not evade it: who does Jesus say is our neighbor? One well-known teacher summarized the Lord's point this way: _Our neighbor is anyone whose need we see and whose need we can meet._

Our neighborly obligations begin with those closest to us, but they do not end there. Our deeds of neighbor love are to extend into the world at large, even so far as to include, as noted above, our enemies (see Matt. 5:44). And these deeds can be costly. Unlike the priest and the Levite, the Samaritan refused to look away. He approached his needy neighbor, cared for him, and put himself on the line for him. He went far out of his way to serve this needy man. His actions were proactive rather than merely passive or reactive. His was expensive service, but this was exactly our Lord's point. The deeds of genuine neighbor love will often prove costly.

> Deliberately and precisely [Jesus] made his mission the model of ours, saying "as the Father has sent me, even so I send you." Therefore our understanding of the church's mission must be deduced from our understanding of the Son's.
> —John Stott

Christ calls his church to emulate the Samaritan. We are not to look away from our neighbor's needs, passing by on the other side (Prov. 28:27). We are proactively to seek our neighbor's welfare even when it may be costly. Why? We are to do it as an outworking of our love for, and emulation of, Jesus himself. He loves our neighbor and has refused to pass him by. In his coming into the world Jesus sought out that neighbor and gave himself sacrificially for him. He calls us to follow his example: "Christ also suffered for you, leaving you an example, so that you might follow in his steps" (1 Pet. 2:21).

The Image of God. Every human being is an image bearer of God and as such deserves the best we have to give. Has anyone stated this point more powerfully than C. S. Lewis? In what may be his most often-quoted words, drawn from his essay (originally a sermon) entitled "The Weight of Glory," Lewis explains the regard each of our neighbors deserves:

> It may be possible for each to think too much of his own potential glory hereafter; it is hardly possible for him to think too often or too deeply about that of his neighbor. The load, or weight, or burden of my neighbor's glory should be laid on my back, a load so heavy that only humility can carry it, and the backs of the proud will be broken. It is a serious thing to live in a society of possible gods and goddesses, to remember that the dullest and most uninteresting person you can talk to may one day be a creature, which, if you saw it now, you would be strongly tempted to worship, or else a horror and a corruption such as you now meet, if at all, only in a nightmare. All day long we are, in some degree, helping one another to one or more of these destinations. It is in the light of these overwhelming possibilities, it is with the awe and circumspection proper to them, that we should conduct all our dealings with one another, all friendships, all loves, all play, all politics. There are no *ordinary* people. You have never talked to a mere mortal. Nations, cultures, arts, civilizations—these are mortal, and their life is to ours as the life of a gnat. But it is immortals whom we joke with, work with, marry, snub, and exploit—immortal horrors or everlasting splendours.[4]

The man lying in a pool of blood beside the Jericho road was no "mere mortal." Nor are the desperately needy people of our own time. We dare not look away and pass them by on the other side, avoiding them simply because we can. Is not our Lord the one who "shows no partiality to princes, nor regards the rich more than the poor, for they are all the work of his hands" (Job 34:18–19)? Our neighbors—*those whose need we see and whose need we can meet*—are created and loved by God. Though fallen and sinful like the rest of us, they are of wondrous value to him. They must not be ignored or dehumanized by us. They are Godlike and as such they retain their full human dignity, even when in a reduced state.

Unlike the priest and the Levite, we must not shy away

from their need. Jesus calls us to reach out to our neighbors, caring for them and putting ourselves on the line for them. This can be costly service but the deeds of genuine neighbor love demand no less. "Whoever knows the right thing to do and fails to do it, for him it is sin" (James 4:17).

The call of Jesus is to get as energized about someone else's being the victim of injustice as you are when it's you. In particular, be concerned about injustice to those you might be inclined to overlook.

—John Ortberg

CHAPTER NINE

SERVING THE KINGDOM

The amazing news of the gospel is that men and women, through Christ's atoning death, can now be reconciled to God. But the good news Jesus proclaimed had a fullness beyond salvation and the forgiveness of sins; it also signified the coming of God's kingdom on earth.

—Richard Stearns

How does the gospel call us to action beyond the believing community? A third line of argument focuses on our role as God's "fellow workers" (1 Cor. 3:9). Jesus calls his church to join him in building his kingdom in the world.

If neighbor love raises the question of obedience to the express command of Jesus, the issue of kingdom building strikes to the very meaning of our service. There may be no more important application of the ladder of abstraction than this one: Christ calls us to join *what he is doing in the world*, which alone can give lasting purpose and meaning to *what we do in the world*.

The Bible describes in a variety of ways God's plan for redeeming his creation through Jesus Christ. This is the massive, overarching theme of the Bible, the Big Story we are called to join. If we join that Big Story, Jesus says, the Little Story of our individual experience gains eternal significance. By contributing the details of our lives to what God is doing in the world, those details come to matter for all eternity. If we refuse to join God's Big Story, on the other hand, we relegate our own small lives to futility and insignificance. We waste our personal stories on things that will and can have no lasting consequence.

2 CORINTHIANS 15:19–21

General	Big Story
	God was reconciling the world to himself in Christ.
	Little Story
Specific	*I must be reconciled to God.*

This is the meaning of that central paradox of the Christian faith: "Whoever finds his life will lose it, and whoever loses his life for my sake will find it" (Matt. 10:39). When we give up our lives in the service of God's kingdom, we discover what God intended human life to be: "I came that they may have life and have it abundantly" (John 10:10). When we seek to hold onto our lives, consuming them upon ourselves, we lose them to meaninglessness, disappointment, and eternal irrelevance.

KINGDOM BUILDING

But what does this mean in practice? What does "contributing the details of our lives to what God is doing in the world" look like? What is God's Big Story and what does it mean for us to join it?

Here we launch out onto what has become a tumultuous theological sea. Jesus said to Pilate, "My kingdom is not of this world" (John 18:36). Yet it was into this world he came to inaugurate that kingdom and to call his people to join it. So how are we to think of and contribute to Christ's kingdom? Is it a this-worldly kingdom (earthly, here and now) or an other-worldly kingdom (spiritual, focused on heaven and eternity)? Or is it in some sense both? And if so, how do the two relate to one another?

> It is not so much the case that God has a mission for his church in the world, as that God has a church for his mission in the world. Mission was not made for the church; the church was made for mission—God's mission.
>
> —Christopher Wright

These questions have generated much debate over the centuries, not least during the last few decades. The issues are deep and complex, and we will not resolve them here. But neither will our topic—the role of our deeds in Christ's calling for his people—permit us to escape the core issue of the debate. It has to do with the very nature of the salvation that is in Christ.

Let us pose the issue this way. All sides of the discussion are interested in the biblical concept of salvation. But they do not all agree on what that concept is. Is salvation in the Bible a salvation *from*, or is it a salvation *for*? Does the biblical emphasis fall on what the saved are *escaping* or on what they are *fleeing toward* and *enlisting in*?

SALVATION FROM

A "salvation from" emphasis views the Bible as focusing on God's gracious provisions for the race's greatest problem. In Adam's fall, sin brought God's sentence of judgment upon the entire *cosmos*, including the human race. Our most serious human dilemma, therefore, is that we have become the object of God's wrath. It is a desperate plight, one from which, left to our own devices, we are utterly unable to extricate ourselves. We are spiritually dead, helplessly mired in our sin and trapped in Satan's kingdom of darkness. Unless God in his mercy provides a means of salvation, there can be no escape. We are doomed to a life of futility in this world and perdition in the next.

> Grace and peace to you from God our Father and the Lord Jesus Christ, who gave himself for our sins to rescue us from the present evil age.
> —Gal. 1:3–4 (NIV)

But thanks be to God: he has in Jesus Christ provided us what we could not provide for ourselves. He sent his Son into the world so that he might give himself for sinners. Jesus lived a perfect life and then offered up his spotless sacrifice on the cross in our place. He took our death and condemnation upon himself, so that we, through faith in him, might experience the forgiveness of our sin and entrance into God's kingdom.

Instead of condemnation, then, in Jesus we discover God's acceptance, being clothed with Christ's own righteousness. Instead of death, in Christ we gain new life, and that more abundant. In place of futility, in Christ our lives gain meaning and purpose in his service. Instead of eternal damnation, in him we receive eternal life and the prospect of endless heavenly delight as we spend eternity enjoying the presence of God. This marvelous account is the focus of the "salvation from" emphasis.[1]

SALVATION FOR

A "salvation for" emphasis, by contrast, stresses the kingdom work to which God's people are called. In his coming as Israel's Messiah, Jesus turned the page of history by inaugurating God's kingdom in the world. By his death on the cross and resurrection from the grave, he defeated sin and death and the forces of evil and began the process of restoring the sin-ravaged *cosmos* in general and the human race in particular to what God originally created them to be. This redemptive task, which "addresses every dimension of the problem that sin has created,"[2] will not be completed until Jesus returns. But in the meantime he calls his people to serve as his agents in the redemption process. As Jesus taught his disciples to pray, "Your kingdom come, your will be done, on earth as it is in heaven" (Matt. 6:10).

Following in Christ's footsteps (1 Pet. 2:21), Christians are to join Jesus in building God's kingdom—that realm where God truly reigns—by bringing into the world, in Christ's name, light where there is darkness; comfort where there is suffering; hope where there is despair; justice where there is oppression; nourishment where there is privation; peace where there is conflict; healing where there is sickness; wholeness where there is brokenness; reconciliation where there is alienation; beauty where sin has stained the world. Jesus calls his people to be "salt" (Matt. 5:13) wherever its preserving qualities are needed. In Christ God is redeeming every dimension of his creation and every aspect of human experience, and he calls his redeemed people to serve him by joining sacrificially in that process, extending God's healing touch to every individual and every community—indeed, to the very cosmos itself through our creation care. These are the works to which Jesus calls us in our own generation. Joining him in building his kingdom is what he calls his church both *to* and *for*.[3]

Kingdom Works. Not everything we do, of course, not even every good thing, qualifies as kingdom building. "*Mission*," says John Stott, "is not a word for everything the church does." Nor does it even "cover everything God does in the world. For God the Creator is constantly active in his world in providence, in common grace and in judgment, quite apart from the purposes for which he has sent his Son, his Spirit and his church into the world."[4] That's why it's important, says James Davison Hunter,

> to underscore that while the activity of culture-making has validity before God, this work is not, strictly speaking, redemptive or salvific in character. Where Christians participate in the work of world-building they are not, in any precise sense of the phrase, "building the kingdom of God." This side of heaven, the culture cannot become the kingdom of God, nor will all the work of Christians in the culture evolve into or bring about his kingdom.[5]

Kingdom work is that done in obedience to, and in the name of, the King. In the New Testament it was for the sake of Jesus's name that his followers went out into the world (3 John 7). It was in that name that they prayed and were empowered (John 14:13–14; 15:16; 16:23, 26). It was by that name that they spoke with boldness, brought healing, and performed miracles (Acts 3:6, 16; 4:7, 10, 30; see also Mark 16:17). It was on account of that name they were persecuted (Luke 21:12) and through that name that they were protected (John 17:11). So powerful was their kingdom work in the name of Jesus that others coveted it and falsely sought to claim it for themselves (Matt. 7:22; 24:5; Mark 9:38–39; 13:6; Luke 9:39; Acts 19:13).

Kingdom building, whether in word or deed, is work done in the name of Jesus Christ. It is Christ-centered work, for there can be no kingdom without the King. Kingdom deeds are those where we stand in Christ's stead (in his name), extending his salvific and redeeming work in the world. One day, at the "name that is above every name," every knee will bow and every tongue confess that Jesus Christ is Lord, "to the glory of God the Father" (Phil. 2:9–11). In the meantime, we confess that name in the world today and work in its power to do *the King's* work until he comes.

> It is in our servant role that we can find the right synthesis of evangelism and social action. For both should be for us, as they undoubtedly were for Christ, authentic expressions of the love that serves.
> —John Stott

Kingdom work is thus not to be confused with those generic deeds of world making and culture building that God designed for the just and unjust alike at creation. The world is not the kingdom, and efforts to make the world a better place do not inherently qualify as kingdom work. By God's common grace, atheists and followers of other gods often work to make the world a better place, but they are not, in so doing, building *Christ's* kingdom. His is a kingdom of light furthered by those whom God has "delivered . . . from the domain of darkness and transferred . . . to the kingdom of his beloved Son" (Col.1:13–14). Christ's kingdom work is that which is accomplished expressly, if not always explicitly, in the name of Jesus.

SALVATION FROM OR SALVATION FOR?

So must we choose between these options, salvation *from* or salvation *for*? Surely not; both emphases are biblical.[6] Yet one might never imagine it in listening to their respective proponents.

In the introduction we noted the so-called lifeboat theology of the nineteenth- and early twentieth-century fundamentalists. These salvation-from advocates seemed blind to the salvation-for dimensions of the church's calling. They were so focused on saving souls for a distant heaven that they grew oblivious to what God is doing in the world today. In their view the cosmos was irredeemable and disposable, one day to be replaced entirely by an other-worldly eternal realm. God's kingdom, it seemed to them, is spiritual, without remainder. Thus concerns for social action in this world were viewed as the refuge of theological liberals who had abandoned the heart of the gospel. It amounted to little more than rearranging the chairs on deck of the Titanic. The church's task, they seemed to think, was solely to rescue men and women from this sinking ship and win them for eternity.

Can such a lifeboat theology still be found today? It can, and advocates of the salvation-for emphasis are right to call it into question. But by the same token, those who stress the importance of the church's kingdom deeds sometimes fall into the opposite error.

> You shall call his name Jesus, for he will save his people from their sins.
> —Matt. 1:21

Our Contemporary Problem. Our generation, it is sometimes said, shows little interest in issues of righteousness, sin, judgment, and forgiveness, so a salvation-from message no longer holds much appeal. People today respond better to a positive message than a negative one. In any case, a salvation-from focus is deemed too individualistic, too obsessed with mere fire insurance. Some will go so far as to insist that such a personalistic emphasis actually misrepresents the gospel. The gospel is about God in Christ redeeming the cosmos, not a system of how people get saved.

But surely this represents a false choice. Let us listen again to C. S. Lewis. In his essay "God in the Dock" (the dock being the place of the accused in a British courtroom),

Lewis famously portrayed moderns as reversing the roles of God and humans:

> The ancient man approached God (or even the gods) as the accused person approaches his judge. For the modern man the roles are reversed. He is the judge: God is in the dock. He is quite a kindly judge: if God should have a reasonable defence for being the god who permits war, poverty and disease, he is ready to listen to it. The trial may even end in God's acquittal. But the important thing is that Man is on the Bench and God in the Dock.[7]

Lewis was no doubt right that many today have lost any real sense of their sinful plight before the bench of a righteous and holy God, more so now than when Lewis published these words (1948). But this scarcely permits us to dismiss this crucial element from our verbal witness, much less from our thinking. Our generation's predicament has not changed and we must not allow its widespread obliviousness to that predicament to infect our own thinking. The fact is, the New Testament brims with a salvation-from emphasis. The apostle Paul considered the affirmation "Christ died for our sins" to be "of first importance" in the gospel (1 Cor. 15:3). By this gospel "you are being saved," he said to the Corinthians, "unless you believed in vain" (v. 2). The issue of individual sin and judgment and salvation is simply inescapable in the apostolic writings.

It is worth asking, in fact, whether the human experience today is really so different after all. The apostle's assessment in Romans 1 remains profoundly relevant. Thus it has been and thus it will ever be: "For since the creation of the world God's invisible qualities—his eternal power and divine nature—have been clearly seen, being understood from what has been made, so that men are without excuse" (v. 20 NIV). Yet like those before it, our generation continues to suppress the truth about God (v. 18), neither glorifying him as God nor giving thanks to him (v. 21), preferring instead to exchange the truth of God for a lie so as to worship and serve the creature rather than the Creator (v. 25). So what's new? Previous generations of God's people have not used these perennial human tendencies to justify eviscerating the gospel message, and neither should we.

The deeper reality is, in our generation as in every other there remain many who are desperate for the liberating word of God's forgiveness. The Hound of Heaven is after them.[8] They intuitively identify with the classic struggle of Bunyan's pilgrim. Like him, and regardless of what their contemporaries may tell them, they experience their sin as an unbearable burden due to the convicting work of the Holy Spirit (John 16:8–11). They long, often without the language to express it, for the emancipation so powerfully described by Charles Wesley:

> Long my imprisoned spirit lay,
> Fast bound in sin and nature's night;
> Thine eye diffused a quick'ning ray,
> I woke, the dungeon flamed with light;
> My chains fell off, my heart was free;
> I rose, went forth and followed Thee.[9]

Whatever else the gospel is about, it is inevitably about the eternal destiny of individuals. The apostle Peter viewed the "salvation of [our] souls [*psuche*]" as the very "goal" (*telos*) of the faith (1 Pet. 1:9 NIV). "For God so loved the world, that he gave his only Son, that whoever believes in him should not perish but have eternal life" (John 3:16). Will I perish? Or will I find eternal life, rescued "from the wrath to come" through Jesus Christ? (1 Thess. 1:10). These individualistic questions lie at the core of the Christian faith. To write them off as a misguided obsession with "fire insurance" is to dismiss something that stands at the center of the biblical gospel.

> This righteousness from God comes through faith in Jesus Christ to all who believe. There is no difference, for all have sinned and fall short of the glory of God, and are justified freely by his grace through the redemption that came by Christ Jesus.
>
> —Rom. 3:22–24 (NIV)

A focus on the believer's eschatological destiny is an inherent part of "the faith and love that spring from the hope that is stored up for you in heaven and that you have already heard about in the word of truth, the gospel that has come to you" (Col. 1:5–6 NIV). The crucial doctrine of bodily resurrection, both Christ's and ours (1 Corinthians 15), is focused intensely on the individual's eternal destiny. No message that plays down this decisive issue can call itself the apostolic gospel.

CONCLUSION

Rather than remaining aloof from, much less contributing to, the world's problems, the church is called to be part of their Christ-centered solution. We are to model for our broken world what God's kingdom looks like, doing whatever we are able to spread its peace and justice and love. We are not only witnesses to that kingdom; we are participants in it and agents of it.

This does not mean, of course, that we have embraced utopianism. The Bible makes short work of any such misguided notion. Nor does it imply some form of post-millennialism wherein we render the world finally worthy of Christ's return. It may well be, as Walter Brueggemann has said, that "the central vision of world history in the Bible is that all of creation is one, every creature in community with every other, living in harmony and security toward the joy and well-being of every other creature."[10] But this can be true only if the world history we have in mind includes Christ's second advent and its aftermath. The full realization of such a magnificent vision of the kingdom must await the return of the King. Only he can bring about the conditions, including his righteous judgment ("from thence he shall come to judge the living and the dead," says the ancient creed), that will make the fulfillment of such a grand vision achievable. In the meantime, we must be about his business, the body of Christ serving as his hands and feet and voice in our own generation, fulfilling the words and deeds of his kingdom until he comes.

CHAPTER TEN

ADORNING THE GOSPEL

What did the first Christian generations know about loving one another and loving the stranger that made their sense of the gospel so irresistible?

—Gordon MacDonald

Kingdom building, neighbor love, and godly wisdom all call us to nonverbal forms of witness in the world at large, Christ-honoring deeds that are worthy of the gospel. These first three lines of thought point naturally to a fourth: by living out the gospel in our *nonverbal* witness, we provide the best possible platform for our *verbal* witness.

> You are the light of the world. . . . Let your light shine before others, so that they may see your good works and give glory to your Father who is in heaven.
> —Matt. 5:14–16

The second chapter of Paul's letter to Titus focuses on some of the behavioral dimensions of our calling. Moving up and down the ladder of abstraction, the apostle offers practical instructions about how to live a gospel-worthy life, or as he puts it, a life that "accords with sound doctrine" (v. 1). His counsel focuses on what Christians are to do and to be. God's people should be temperate, and kind, and self-controlled, he says. We are to be people who are careful to honor the Lord with our speech. We should not be liars, or thieves, or slanderers, or drunkards. Instead we are to be people of integrity, people who can be fully trusted, people who are genuinely worthy of respect.

Why are we to be and do these things? Dispersed throughout his practical instructions the apostle offers three purpose statements that are instructive. We are to live this way, he says,

- [so] that the word of God may not be reviled (v. 5);
- so that an opponent may be put to shame, having nothing evil to say about us (v. 8; see also 1 Pet. 3:16);
- so that in every way they will make the teaching about God our Savior attractive (v. 10 NIV).

These purpose statements echo our Lord's exhortation to "let your light shine before others, so that they may see your good works and give glory to your Father who is in heaven" (Matt. 5:16; see also 1 Cor. 6:3). How we live, our behavior—the nonverbal dimension of what we communicate to others—exerts a profound influence on what others will think, not only of us but of the one we proclaim. If the communication of the gospel itself requires the verbal code, the various nonverbal codes incessantly convey the rest of our message, and it's a function they perform exceedingly well. It is sobering to be confronted so directly with the reality that, according to the apostle Paul, our deeds bear the capacity to render the gospel of Jesus Christ attractive—or the reverse.

SOURCE CREDIBILITY

Over three hundred years before Paul, Aristotle wrote a widely used treatise on the art of persuasion. In that work he famously identified "the available means of persuasion" as *logos*, *pathos*, and *ethos*. The first two correspond roughly to what we think of as logical arguments and emotional appeals. The third, *ethos*, addresses "the personal character of the speaker."

Some of Aristotle's predecessors had argued that issues of character play little part in the persuasive process. Aristotle strongly disagreed. "We believe good men more fully and more readily than others," he claimed.

> It is not true, as some writers assume in their treatises on rhetoric, that the personal goodness revealed by the speaker contributes nothing to his power of persuasion; on the contrary, his character may almost be called the most effective means of persuasion he possesses.[1]

Aristotle was referring here primarily to the way speakers generate source credibility within the speech itself, but his point holds more broadly. We do indeed tend to give more credence to those we perceive to be "good" people. This is why our *deeds* form such a crucial backdrop for our *words*.

VERBAL AND NONVERBAL INTERACTION

In an earlier chapter we observed that the verbal and nonverbal dimensions of our communication typically interact in five ways: *repeating, complementing, substituting, contradicting, and regulating.* When the subject is the church's verbal witness of the gospel, two of these categories drop out. Neither *substituting* nor *repeating* applies; our deeds cannot substitute for or actually repeat the verbal witness of the gospel. The other three categories, however, apply directly to the verbal and nonverbal aspects of our calling.

Complementing. As the apostle Paul reminds us, our deeds can supplement our verbal witness. They can bring credit to the gospel by affecting how it is heard. If those deeds cannot themselves preach the gospel, they can certainly grace it and render us more believable as its messengers, thereby "adorning" (*kosmeo*, "to embellish with honor, to dignify," Titus 2:10) the word we preach.

> Gunmen killed 10 medical workers, including eight foreigners, in Afghanistan's remote northeast, police and officials said on Saturday, and the Taliban claimed responsibility for the attack. A Christian aid group said those killed matched descriptions of members of one of its mobile eye clinics who had been traveling in northeasten Nuristan province and were heading back to Kabul after providing medical care for local Afghans.
> —Reuters, August 7, 2010

Regulating. Our nonverbal messages often influence, for good or ill, our ability to communicate the verbal message. Deeds can erect barriers, or they can open doors. The more credible we become, the more open our listeners may be to our verbal witness. To be sure, Jesus warned that, the world being what it is, there are no guarantees. Doors may close no matter how faithfully we fulfill the deeds of Christ's kingdom. In fact, opportunities for verbal witness sometimes close precisely *because* of our good deeds, as when Christian aid workers are killed or expelled somewhere in the world because hostile forces have found their nonverbal Christian witness too effective to tolerate. But history will testify that the church's deeds of authentic neighbor love have often expanded its opportunities for verbal witness.

Contradicting. Or the reverse. Sadly, this has also been the case. Our deeds, or the lack of them in the right situation, can contradict and discredit the message we preach. Our actions speak so loudly the world cannot hear, or becomes unwilling to hear, what we have to say. Unloving people speaking about

Christ's love lack credibility. By their deeds they bring his gospel into disrepute.

We simply cannot not communicate. Our nonverbal messages give us away. Our deeds are constantly working together with our verbal message, rendering it more or less credible. They form the inevitable context within which our verbal message is heard.

GOSPEL-WORTHY DEEDS

Deeds that are gospel-worthy—that is, deeds that are the *enactment* of the gospel, complementing and reinforcing it— begin with those closest to us, our families and our fellow believers. Jesus said, "Just as I have loved you, you also are to love one another. By this all people will know that you are my disciples, if you have love for one another" (John 13:34–35).

A failure to love those closest to us grievously contradicts the gospel, draining believability from our witness. Mismanaging their own homes, for example, undermines the credibility of those who seek to lead the church (1 Tim. 3:4–5). Discord, dissensions, and factions in the church, certain evidence of "the flesh" (Gal. 5:19), discredit the gospel. Where the Spirit is at work there is "love, joy, peace, patience, kindness, goodness, faithfulness, gentleness, self-control" (vv. 22–23). Believers manifesting these traits toward one another have always arrested the world's attention.

It was these very qualities, for example, that the Athenian philosopher Aristides cited in what amounted to an evangelistic appeal to the Roman emperor Hadrian (ca. AD 125). Speaking of the Christians he said:

> They do not worship strange gods, and they go their way in all modesty and cheerfulness. Falsehood is not found among them; and they love one another, and from widows they do

not turn away their esteem; and they deliver the orphan from him who treats him harshly. And he, who has, gives to him who has not, without boasting. And when they see a stranger, they take him in to their homes and rejoice over him as a very brother; for they do not call them brethren after the flesh, but brethren after the spirit and in God. And whenever one of their poor passes from the world, each one of them according to his ability gives heed to him and carefully sees to his burial. And if they hear that one of their number is imprisoned or afflicted on account of the name of their Messiah, all of them anxiously minister to his necessity, and if it is possible to redeem him they set him free. And if there is among them any that is poor and needy, and if they have no spare food, they fast two or three days in order to supply to the needy their lack of food. They observe the precepts of their Messiah with much care, living justly and soberly as the Lord their God commanded them.[2]

In a similar vein, Tertullian (ca. AD 160–220), perhaps the leading Latin father of the early church and an ardent defender of his fellow believers, challenged those who accused the church of mishandling money. In doing so, he provided another glimpse of what it meant for early church believers to love one another:

There is no buying and selling of any sort in the things of God. Though we have our treasure-chest, it is not made up of purchase-money, as of a religion that has its price. On the monthly day, if he likes, each puts in a small donation; but only if it be his pleasure, and only if he be able: for there is no compulsion; all is voluntary. These gifts are, as it were, piety's deposit fund. For they are not taken thence and spent on feasts, and drinking-bouts, and eating-houses, but to support and bury poor people, to supply the wants of boys and girls destitute of means and parents, and of old persons confined now to the house; such, too, as have suffered shipwreck; and if there happen to be any in the mines, or banished to the islands, or shut up in the prisons, for nothing but their fidelity to the cause of God's Church, they become the nurslings of their confession. But it is mainly the deeds of a love so noble that lead many to put a brand upon us. See, they say, how they love one another, . . . how they are ready even to die for one another.[3]

Beyond the Church. How Christians care for those closest to them, or fail to do so, has always set the context for their proclamation of the gospel. But so have their actions *beyond* the boundaries of the church. For example, consider the unexpected testimony of Julian the Apostate.

Julian was a fourth-century Roman emperor who was raised as a Christian. After becoming emperor he turned away from the faith (hence the label "apostate") in an effort to take the empire back to its ancient Roman religious practices. He complained bitterly, however, that the Christians were making his task difficult. Their widespread care for the poor, he said, both reinforced the gospel they preached and undermined the credibility of the Roman religion:

> While the pagan priests neglect the poor, the hated Galileans [Christians] devote themselves to works of charity, and by a display of false compassion have established and given effect to their pernicious errors. See their love-feasts, and their tables spread for the indigent. Such practice is common among them, and causes a contempt for our gods.

Or consider this account from our own generation. A 2008 column in *The Times* of London by self-described atheist Matthew Parris provided an exceptionally candid glimpse of how believers may adorn the gospel.[4] In this column Parris applauds the social action of Christians in Africa over the years (hospitals, education, clean water, etc.); these contributions are obvious to all, he says. But then he digs deeper. With resignation, but also admirable honesty, Parris tells the story of some other far more subtle but equally profound dimensions of the Christians' nonverbal witness in Africa.

Keep your conduct among the Gentiles honorable, so that when they speak against you as evildoers, they may see your good deeds and glorify God on the day of visitation.

—1 Pet. 2:12

Parris grew up in Africa and had traveled widely across the continent. Now, in his later years, he was returning to Africa to observe the work of one particular development agency. This visit refreshed in him a reluctant conviction he confesses he'd "been trying to banish all my life," but which he had "been unable to avoid since my African childhood." It was a conviction, he says, that "confounds my ideological beliefs, stubbornly refuses to fit my world view, and has embarrassed my growing belief that there is no God." What was this conviction?

> Now a confirmed atheist, I've become convinced of the enormous contribution that Christian evangelism makes in Africa. . . . Education and training alone will not do. In Africa Christianity changes people's hearts. It brings a spiritual transformation. The rebirth is real. The change is good.

As a boy Parris had known Christian missionaries and stayed with them. He had also known native African Christians:

> The Christians were always different. Far from having cowed or confined its converts, their faith appeared to have liberated and relaxed them. There was a liveliness, a curiosity, an engagement with the world—a directness in their dealings with others—that seemed to be missing in traditional African life.

Later, Parris observed the same thing when he crisscrossed Africa with some friends. "Whenever we entered a territory worked by missionaries, we had to acknowledge that something changed in the faces of the people we passed and spoke to." What Parris observed was something intangible, "something in their eyes, the way they approached you direct, man-to-man, without looking down or away." The Christians seemed more secure, more open.

This was the impression that was refreshed upon his return to Africa, now forty-five years later. The most impressive African members of the secular agency he was visiting turned out to be Christians. "It would suit me," Parris says, "to believe that their honesty, diligence and optimism in their work was unconnected with personal faith." Instead, Parris was forced to acknowledge that the work of these Christians, while secular, was deeply affected by what they were. And "what they were was, in turn, influenced by a conception of man's place in the Universe that Christianity had taught."

Parris's account is a useful reminder that the "deeds" which form the backdrop for the verbal gospel reach far beyond the obvious. Standing up for justice in the world and spending ourselves in acts of mercy and compassion are obvious and often costly aspects of our nonverbal witness. Parris had always been begrudgingly impressed by such visible expressions of Christian love—deeds, he says, "only the severest kind of secularist" could deny. But what also caught his attention and forced his admiration were those far more ordinary, mundane, daily deeds of the believers—their honesty, integrity, diligence, transparency, and optimism—which Parris recognized as expressions of what it means to live for Christ in the world. These too constitute the gospel-worthy conduct that sets the context for how our verbal witness will be heard.

THE DEEDS OF DAILY LIFE

I was struck by these everyday connections in an incident that occurred while we were on vacation with friends. The husband realized one evening that sometime during the day he had lost his billfold. It contained his driver's license, all his credit cards, and a significant amount of cash. He was suddenly faced with the loss of his identification, the inability to drive a vehicle until he could secure a temporary license, the necessity of having to cancel all his credit cards, and the loss of a sizable amount of money.

Thinking back over his day, my friend determined that the last place he had seen his wallet was at the golf course. He decided he had either left his wallet in the golf cart or inadvertently dropped it in the parking lot. He called the course immediately, but by this time the office was closed, and the phone went unanswered.

The following morning we were the first ones in the parking lot. After a brief look around, without result, my friend entered the clubhouse and asked whether anyone had turned in his billfold. As it happened, someone had found it lying on the ground in the parking lot the previous day and brought it in. My friend recovered his wallet intact, with not a dollar missing.

This happy result may reflect something pleasant about golf, a game in which players routinely call fouls on themselves. There was probably a better chance of recovering an intact billfold from a golf course parking lot than many another location we can imagine. But my point in recounting this incident is not to valorize golf. It has to do with the relationship between our kingdom deeds and words.

Imagine two very different people discovering this billfold lying on the ground. The first picks it up, looks around, and discovers no one paying attention. He moves over into the shadows and rifles through the wallet. He realizes he has just hit the jackpot. The identification and credit cards are of no use to him because he's unwilling to chance being caught using them. But the cash is a different story. Figuring it's a case of finders-keepers, he looks around again and then pockets the cash. "If a guy can't keep track of his own wallet," he says to himself, "he deserves to lose it." After discarding the rest in a nearby trash container, he walks away hundreds of dollars richer.

Now imagine a different fellow finding the wallet. This one opens it and immediately sees that it contains someone's identification, credit cards, and a large amount of cash. His first thought is, "Whoa, someone is really going to be missing this." He imagines the sense of panic he would experience if he lost his own billfold this way and pictures the wallet's owner in a similar state. He also realizes how relieved and grateful he would be if he were to recover his wallet intact. It delights him to think that he can make this happen for the one whose things he holds in his hands. How best to accomplish that? The owner will most likely come back to the golf course looking for it, he says to himself, so it will be best to turn the billfold in to the staff in the pro shop. He does so, and then walks away wishing he could be there to see the joy and relief on the face of the wallet's owner when he discovers all is well.

These two responses represent polar opposites. The first is quintessentially *self*-ish; that is, it's about the *self*. The focus from the outset is about "me." The "other" and his needs are irrelevant; in fact, invisible. The only question is how the situation can best be used to enrich himself without incurring risk.

The second response is the reverse. There is a selflessness about the man's reaction. His first thought is not for himself but for the wallet's owner. His deliberations are marked by empathy for what the *other* is experiencing, and his course of action is dictated by what is in the *other's* best interest. His is the response not only of integrity but of Christian love.

> Christians need to look like what they are talking about.
> —John Poulton

Finally, imagine an unbelieving owner of such a wallet later being introduced to the one who returned it, and the returner somehow having an opportunity to share the gospel with the wallet's owner. What would be the effect of the returner's deeds on how the owner might hear his words? How might his act of neighbor love "adorn" that verbal witness in the ears of the man who recovered his wallet intact? The listener might well find himself eager to understand what motivated such a remarkable display of selflessness, love, and integrity.

Does the world see Christ's church in these terms? Do our personal lives adorn the gospel we preach? Do our corporate deeds reflect such a consistent concern for the "other" that a watching world is curious to hear what motivates us? Does our way of life render attractive the King we serve and the kingdom we claim to inhabit? Can it truly be said of us that we love our neighbors as ourselves?

CONCLUSION

The church's mission in the world is both *verbal* and *nonverbal*. The two dimensions play complementary roles, and neither can substitute for the other.

Some seem to enjoy calling for the elimination of any such dualism. "This is modernity speaking," they will say; "we must transcend all such of dualistic thinking." It's a trendy thought but also misguided. There are unfortunate dichotomies to be avoided in our thinking, but this is not one of them. Not all distinctions represent false dualisms, and it's a prescription for confusion to write them off as if they do. Some distinctions are not only valid; they are crucial, and the distinction between our verbal and nonverbal witness is one of those. Collapsing these two into one is simply a case of glossing over the obvious.

Christ's call upon his church claims all of our lives, our *deeds* as well as our *words*. Part of our calling is to love our neighbors and do the works of Christ's kingdom. These good works will not, and cannot, replace our verbal witness. Nor are they dispensable. They constitute the essential context in which our verbal witness is heard. They are the nonverbal message the world receives from us, which significantly shapes how they hear our verbal message.

There is a classic account of two farmers out surveying a field. Experienced farmers view a well-cultivated field as a work of art. The one said to the other, "You and the Lord certainly have a beautiful field here." To which the second replied, "Yes, but you should have seen it when the Lord had it to himself."

> But among us you will find uneducated persons, and artisans, and old women, who, if they are unable in words to prove the benefit of our doctrine, yet by their deeds exhibit the benefit arising from their persuasion of its truth: they do not rehearse speeches, but exhibit good works; when struck, they do not strike again; when robbed, they do not go to law; they give to those that ask of them, and love their neighbors as themselves.
> —Athenagoras (AD 133–190), *Plea for the Christians*

Despite its flippant tone, this response embodies an important biblical truth. Speaking of his own kingdom work the apostle Paul said, "I planted the seed, Apollos watered it, but God made it grow" (1 Cor. 3:6 NIV). Only God can generate the growth, but he has chosen to use our kingdom words and deeds in the process.

We have a God-ordained role to play. The gospel does not lose its power when we fail to do our part or fulfill it poorly; that power is ultimately the result of the Spirit's intent to use the good news of what God has done, is doing, and will do in Jesus Christ to draw men and women to himself. The only question is what role we will play in that process. Will we help or hinder? God could have ordered it otherwise, but he has graciously designed us into the work of building his kingdom, by both our words and deeds. It is our task to be faithful to that twofold calling.

CHAPTER ELEVEN

STEWARDING THE CREATION

Humans are thoroughly relational, inextricably related to and bound up not only with God, and not only with other human beings, but also with the animals and plants, the microbes and mountains of this exquisitely complex and beautiful blue-green earth.

—Steven Bouma-Prediger

How does the gospel call us to action in our fifth circle of application, the created order?

It is unfortunate that this has become such a hot topic in our generation. Many Christians are skeptical of the notion that the gospel has anything to say about their ecological behavior. Others are outright hostile to the idea. At the other end of the continuum are those who believe the demands of the gospel translate directly into a specific set of national and international policies on the environment in general and climate change in particular. And in between are a great many well-intentioned Christians who don't know quite what to think.

The reason for this state of affairs, I suspect, is again partly due to the fact that, like our fourth circle of application, society at large, the Scriptures have little to say in any direct way about what gospel-worthy conduct looks like in this fifth circle, the natural creation. Yet the difficulty here may be even greater. It may be that in this realm Christians not only must work out for themselves the appropriate applications; the deeper reality is that they lack a clear grasp of the more abstract truths or principles they are called to apply. Hence their confusion about what's required of them as gospel-minded Christians.

What are the more abstract, higher-order biblical teachings about the created order that we should be seeking to implement in our behavior as God's people? In other words, how does the gospel call us to action in this fifth circle of application?

GOD'S VICE-REGENTS

The Bible teaches that, having completed his creation and deemed it "good," God assigned humans the role of his vice-regents in the world: "God said to them, 'Be fruitful and multiply and fill the earth and subdue it, and have dominion over the fish of the sea and over the birds of the heavens and over every living thing that moves on the earth'" (Gen. 1:28). This assignment has led some to speak of humanity's so-called cultural mandate or creation mandate. God designed men and women to serve as stewards of his creation, to manage it on his behalf.

Unfortunately, in the fall (Genesis 3) "the creation was subjected to frustration" due to sin and "has been groaning as in the pains of childbirth right up to the present time" (Rom. 8:20, 22 NIV). This cosmic "frustration" (*mataiotes*, "vanity," "futility") has been from the beginning complicated by humanity's sinful tendencies, which have often led to the selfish exploitation of the creation rather than a careful, sustainable stewardship. The result has been the repeated degradation of the earth rather than its flourishing.

But, thankfully, God is not through with his creation. He loves the world he created, and his purpose is not to discard it as refuse. In Christ he is redeeming not just the human race but the entire fallen universe.

> The scope of divine redemption is not just the saving of lost souls but the renewing of life as a whole, and beyond that, the renewing of all creation.
> —Nicholas Wolterstorff

One day, according to the apostle Paul, "the creation itself will be set free from its bondage to corruption" (Rom. 8:21). But in order for that to happen it will have to experience its own form of death and resurrection. First, it must die: "The heavens will pass away with a roar, and the heavenly bodies will be burned up and dissolved, and the earth and the works that are done on it will be exposed. . . . The heavens will be set on fire and dissolved, and the heavenly bodies will melt as they burn!" (2 Pet. 3:10–12). But then from this refining fire will emerge a new heavens and a new earth (Revelation 21–22), one which will constitute the dwelling place of God's people throughout eternity. According to 1 Corinthians 15:35–58, this renewed world will be a physical place where God's people will dwell in resurrected, glorified bodies modeled after Christ's. This will be the sin-free place where the Lord "will wipe every tear from their eyes. There will be no more death or mourning or crying or pain, for the old order of things has passed away" (Rev. 21:4 NIV; see also Isa. 25:8). And so shall we be "at home with the Lord" forever (2 Cor. 5:8; 1 Thess. 4:17).

Notice in this biblical account of God's plan for the world that while sin and its effects are bad, the created order itself is good. The Bible knows nothing of the ancient Greek suspicion that material things are inherently evil. What's more, our eternal destiny is not to escape our bodies and the material realm in order to dwell with God as spirits in some ethereal heavenly realm; on the contrary, both our bodies and the material world will be made new in the resurrection and consummation of all things.

A DRAMATIC TRANSFORMATION

In their effort to emphasize the continuity between the present world and the next and to combat common but unbiblical, even heretical, images of our eternal dwelling place (e.g., humans having become angels with harps floating on heavenly clouds), Christian environmentalists have sometimes understated the creation's dramatic transition from the old to the new. But the writer to the Hebrews stressed the opposite. In his argument from the lesser to the greater, he vividly compared this cataclysmic future transformation to the fearful events that accompanied the giving of the Mosaic Law. In coming to Mount Sinai, he says, the terrified Israelites were approaching:

> a blazing fire and darkness and gloom and a tempest and the sound of a trumpet and a voice whose words made the hearers beg that no further messages be spoken to them. For they could not endure the order that was given, "If even a beast touches the mountain, it shall be stoned." Indeed, so terrifying was the sight that Moses said, "I tremble with fear." (Heb. 12:18–21)

Yet that terrifying scene was nothing, says the author of Hebrews, compared to what is yet to come:

> At that time his voice shook the earth, but now he has promised, "Yet once more I will shake not only the earth but also the heavens." This phrase, "Yet once more," indicates the removal of things that are shaken—that is, things that have been made—in order that the things that cannot be shaken

may remain. Therefore let us be grateful for receiving a kingdom that cannot be shaken, and thus let us offer to God acceptable worship, with reverence and awe, for our God is a consuming fire. (vv. 26–29)

The making of the *new* heavens and earth will not be a light rehab. Only that which is eternal will make it through the fire. The transformation to the new requires the dying of the old. Jesus spelled out the principle in John 12:24 when he said, "Unless a kernel of wheat falls to the ground and dies, it remains only a single seed" (NIV). The apostle Paul then applied this principle to the bodily resurrection of the believer:

What you sow does not come to life unless it dies. And what you sow is not the body that is to be, but a bare kernel, perhaps of wheat or of some other grain. . . . So is it with the resurrection of the dead. What is sown is perishable; what is raised is imperishable. It is sown in dishonor; it is raised in glory. It is sown in weakness; it is raised in power. It is sown a natural body; it is raised a spiritual body. (1 Cor. 15:36–37, 42–44)

In the same way, the old creation will one day die in the refining fire of God's judgment (see Matt. 5:18; Mark 13:31) and emerge from the flames as the new heavens and the new earth, "a radical and thoroughgoing renovation of the world as we now know it."[1] Just as our Lord's resurrected body was a glorified, eternal version of his earthly body, so too will the believer's body be. And so too will the new heavens and earth be a glorified, refashioned version of the old. "Then comes the end, when [Christ] delivers the kingdom to God the Father" (1 Cor. 15:24).

GOSPEL-WORTHY BEHAVIOR

"Since everything will be destroyed in this way, what kind of people ought you to be?" asked Peter (2 Pet. 3:11 NIV). What sort of implications does the above account bear for how we are to live in the world? Peter's answer focused on the first circle of application, our personal lives: "You ought to live holy and godly lives as you look forward to the day of God and speed its coming" (vv. 11–12 NIV). But it's not difficult to see that this biblical scenario bears implications for the other circles as well.

> The earth is the LORD's, and everything in it, the world, and all who live in it.
> —Ps. 24:1 (NIV)

If the above is God's eternal plan for the cosmos, it's clear that he is not through with what he has made. He repeatedly declared what he had created to be good, and just as the fall did not render humans worthless to God, neither did it render the creation worthless. God values the created order and placed us here as its custodians.

When we were yet in our sins, we may have known little about, and cared even less for, God's heart for the creation and the stewardship he envisioned for the human race. But as those who have experienced God's redeeming grace in Jesus Christ and have set out to serve him as Lord, we can no longer remain oblivious to God's desires for the creation. If the human race in general has largely defaulted in its stewardship role, God's people must not blindly follow along. They must ask what this stewardship requires of them and then seek to live it out. God's natural creation too is one of the circles of application where we are called to gospel-worthy behavior.

> The earth is the property of the God we claim to love and obey. We care for the earth, most simply, because it belongs to the one whom we call Lord.
> —"The Cape Town Commitment," 2011

What specifically does this require? The issues are thorny and, with the apparent warming of the earth's climate, increasingly urgent. Terms such as *global warming*, *carbon footprint*, *renewable resources*, *green revolution*, and *cap and trade* have become part of our everyday parlance. A covert pantheism or a not-so-covert materialism often seems to be driving the various environmentalist agendas. On the other hand, Christian thinkers are doing an ever-better job of addressing the issues from the Bible, challenging our unbridled consumerism (see Heb. 13:5–6) and calling us, for all the right biblical reasons, to a more sustainable way of living.[2]

> One question for any kind of activism is, how long are you going to be able to keep doing it? If you believe you're going to be able, by technology, by political force, by whatever means, to save the planet, you may well get exhausted and disillusioned and depressed. . . . If, on the other hand, you do what you do because you believe it pleases the living God, who is the Creator and whose handiwork this is, your perspective is very different. . . . . [I] believe it gives God tremendous pleasure when his people do what they were created to do. Which is care for what he made.
>
> —Peter Harris

We cannot, of course, attempt to work out the many issues here. That would require a different book, even were I the right person to write it. For our purposes we must settle for something less. I wish to emphasize only the simple but inescapable conclusion that when the apostle Paul exhorts us to conduct ourselves in a manner "worthy of the gospel of Christ" (Phil. 1:27), this inevitably bears implications for how we relate not only to other people but to God's creation. If all of our conduct is to be shaped and informed by our allegiance to Jesus Christ, what does his plan for the world demand of us? What is my part, however humble, in that plan?

It will not do to look away in apathy, as if the issues have nothing to do with me, or to use the misguided notions of others to justify retreating into passivity. What does our God-given stewardship of creation require of us? Different Christians may answer this question differently, with more or less faithfulness to our biblically informed responsibilities to the creation. But the one answer that is surely unacceptable is "Nothing." Christ's gospel must not only be preached; it must be lived by his people. It must be *incarnated* in the concrete details of our lives. So what does gospel-worthy, Christ-honoring care for God's creation look like for you?

PART 3

THE IMPORTANCE OF HANDLING SCRIPTURE WELL

CHAPTER TWELVE

RIGHTLY DIVIDING THE WORD

> I think there are some exegetical mistakes, over-statements, and sloppy thinking being promoted in an effort to arouse our passions for social justice and the poor. Perhaps a careful, slow look at a number of different passages can help put our concern for the poor on more solid footing.
>
> —Kevin DeYoung

Our goal throughout this book has been to offer help in thinking biblically about the enduring question of "word versus deed" in the Christian's calling. This goal has required us to pay close attention to what the Scriptures actually say about our topic. Even the material we have drawn from the field of communication was introduced to help us grasp more clearly what the Bible is teaching.

In this chapter we must do the opposite, so to speak. Our goal here is to address some of the things the Bible does *not* teach, which is to say, some of the common ways the Bible may be misused in this discussion.

When we cite a text of Scripture it is not enough to avoid spouting heresy. It's important that we also avoid attributing things to God that he never said, or at least that he did not say in this particular passage. If God has affirmed something in the Bible, let us turn to where he says it and pay close attention. But we must not foist that message on other unsuspecting texts, no matter how worthwhile we think the message may be. We must treat each passage with integrity and listen as best we can to what it wants to tell us. Otherwise we become textual workmen who do indeed need to be ashamed of our careless handling of the word of truth (2 Tim. 2:15).

In previous chapters we emphasized God's call upon his church to serve him with both deeds *and* words. Yet the worthy goal of urging God's people toward these important tasks cannot justify the misappropriation of Scripture, a phenomenon that is all too common in the "word versus deed" debate. Biblical texts are unwittingly shorn of their context and harnessed in ways that, despite the best of motives, do them a disservice. The following are some of the more common ways the Bible is misused in this discussion.

THE GOSPELS VERSUS THE EPISTLES

Sometimes the witness of the Gospel accounts is given priority over the other New Testament writings or vice versa—a mistake we spoke of in an earlier chapter. Often this boils down to the "Jesus versus the apostles" problem. In this way, instead of allowing both testimonies to play their rightful roles, one of these witnesses is used to trump the other.

This mistake can lead to serious misreadings of the Bible. As we have said, most of the events and teaching recorded in the Gospels predated the climactic death, burial, resurrection, ascension, and exaltation of Jesus, not to mention his paradigm-changing outpouring of the Spirit at Pentecost, his enthronement as head of the church, and the deployment of his handpicked, Spirit-empowered apostles to represent him in the world. To read the Gospels without due attention to these later developments is a prescription for misunderstanding what they have to say to us today.

But the reverse is also true. These later developments

scarcely render the Gospel accounts passé. The Gospels provide far more than mere backstory to the Epistles. The two voices complement one another in the New Testament, and it is a serious mistake to relegate the Gospels, in theory or practice, to a secondary role. We will never understand the Epistles apart from what we can know only from the Gospels. All of the New Testament writings were penned after the middle of the first century, which means that the four Gospels were actually written contemporaneously with or even later than many of the Epistles. Thus the two testimonies were designed to be read together, and we must give them both their due. Together they are focused on who Jesus is and what God has done, is doing, and will do through him in the world.

Jesus's Mission. Those who play Jesus off against Paul in the "word versus deed" discussion are sometimes guilty of missing this point. Paul spoke often of our verbal witness, they will acknowledge, but Jesus's ministry, as described in the Gospels, is portrayed as focusing more on kingdom deeds. The idea seems to be that this should weight the scales in our own understanding of the church's task toward following Jesus's model, elevating deeds over words.

Yet this represents a misreading of the New Testament, a fateful focusing on one part of Scripture at the expense of another, one which moreover does not do justice even to the portion it seeks to champion. The balanced stance we have laid out in the previous chapters is not the product of one part of Scripture alone. Nor did Jesus privilege kingdom deeds even in his own ministry. The Gospels show Jesus following in the train of the prophets by carrying out a balanced ministry that, if anything, privileged his *verbal* witness:

> And when it was day, he departed and went into a desolate place. And the people sought him and came to him, and would have kept him from leaving them, but he said to them, "I must preach the good news of the kingdom of God to the

other towns as well; *for I was sent for this purpose.*" And he was preaching in the synagogues of Judea. (Luke 4:42–44; see also Mark 1:38; Luke 4:18–19)

The apostolic era of the church's history produced both the canonical Gospels and the Epistles, twin testimonies that are designed to be read together. Both give witness to the crucial verbal and nonverbal dimensions of the church's calling. We should view them as complementing rather than competing against one another. Using either to offset the other reflects a serious distortion of Scripture.

OLD TESTAMENT VERSUS NEW TESTAMENT

One of the enduring challenges in biblical interpretation is measuring the continuity and discontinuity between the Old and New Testaments. Everyone acknowledges elements of both, but the question is where to set the proportions. How much is continuous from the Old Testament to the New, and how much is discontinuous?

We dare not try to set these boundaries here. That discussion would take us far afield from our subject. But the issue is relevant to our present discussion in at least one important way. The discussion of "word versus deed" in the church's mission often takes recourse to the Old Testament, and to the Mosaic Law in particular. The goal is to demonstrate God's concern for the poor in society as seen in the law's various provisions for their needs. This is then used to energize our concern for the poor in our own generation.

This move requires a great deal of care if we are to avoid misusing the Bible. The question is not whether God cares for the poor and the vulnerable, the widow and the orphan. We may be certain that he does; this is amply demonstrated everywhere in the Bible. The question we must raise here is a more specific one, having to do with the application of the

Old Testament law to our contemporary situation. This is where the challenge lies.

Israel's Theocracy. The nation of Israel was a theocracy. God was the nation's civil head, and the Mosaic Law was his revealed legal code, directing how his covenant people should live. As such, the law's provisions, including those relating to the poor, were directed mainly to life within the theocratic community (something we noted earlier).

> For there will never cease to be poor in the land. Therefore I command you, "You shall open wide your hand to your brother, to the needy and to the poor, in your land."
> —Deut. 15:11

God's intent for Israel from the outset was that "there will be no poor among you; for the LORD will bless you in the land that the LORD your God is giving you for an inheritance to possess" (Deut. 15:4). Yet God also knew that because of the sinfulness of the human heart there would always be poor people in the land (Deut. 15:11; Matt. 26:11). Thus he instructs the Israelites to be especially generous with their needy brothers and sisters.

The law's provisions for the poor were thus primarily for fellow Israelites, which is to say, fellow members of God's people, our third circle of application. They were directions for how one Israelite was to treat another. In fact, the law often drew an explicit distinction between the Israelites and even those strangers or sojourners who were living among them (e.g., Lev. 25:47; Deut. 24:14; Ezek. 22:29).[1] Israel consistently failed these brotherly obligations, of course (see Psalm 10), resulting in repeated warnings and expressions of judgment through the Jewish prophets (e.g., Isaiah 58). But virtually all of these prophetic instructions were addressed to the theocratic context.[2] They were focused on life within the believing community. They were not directed toward Israel's obligations to the poor beyond the community's boundaries.

The Usury Laws. The law's provisions against usury illustrate this internal focus. Loans in ancient Israel were largely designed to help poor, struggling fellow Israelites, from whom lenders were forbidden to take a profit. But this law did not apply in the same way to nonmembers of the covenant community:

> You shall not charge interest on loans to your brother, interest on money, interest on food, interest on anything that is lent for interest. You may charge a foreigner interest, but you may not charge your brother interest, that the LORD your God may bless you in all that you undertake in the land that you are entering to take possession of it. (Deut. 23:19–20)

The usury laws demonstrate God's regard for the poor, but it was not "the poor" in any generic sense. These laws were directed toward the needs of poor Israelites. This in turn shapes how we must view their relevance for our own setting.

Notice again that the question is not whether God cares for the poor beyond the borders of the believing community. He certainly does. Our point is that this is not the issue these legal passages are addressing. Israel's laws were focused on how one brother was to treat another (see Neh. 5:1–8; Isa. 3:13–15). Hence, carelessly pressing them into broader duty by applying them directly to our obligations to society at large does them a disservice. Shearing a passage from its context is almost always a prescription for misunderstanding and misusing it.

Relevance for Today. Does this mean that because we do not live in a theocracy under the Mosaic Law, such legal passages are irrelevant to us? Certainly not. "All Scripture is breathed out by God and profitable for teaching, for reproof, for correction, and for training in righteousness," so that we may be thoroughly "equipped for every good work" (2 Tim. 3:16–17). "For whatever was written in former days was written for our instruction, that through endurance and through the encouragement of the Scriptures we might have hope" (Rom. 15:4; see also 1 Cor. 10:11). These legal stipulations of the Old Testament remain profoundly relevant to us. But we must not force that relevance by decontextualizing them. Rather, we discover their relevance precisely in what they actually say, in context, not in what we wish them to say.

> The Mosaic laws of social justice are grounded in God's character, and that never changes. . . . If this is true of God, we who believe in him must always find some way of expressing it [in] our own practices, even if believers now live in a new stage in the history of God's redemption.
> —Tim Keller

In this instance, the relevance of these legal passages for us lies first in the subject to which they are dedicated: life within the believing community. They are immediately pertinent to the discussion of how Christians are to relate to their fellow Christians, not as law now but by providing insight into God's heart for his people and their life together. As such they serve as a foundation for the extensive instructions in the New Testament on this subject. They speak to us eloquently of the sort of loving care God's people are to show one another. Consider, for example, the brotherly sensitivity enjoined in passages such as this:

> When you make your neighbor a loan of any sort, you shall not go into his house to collect his pledge. You shall stand outside, and the man to whom you make the loan shall bring

THE IMPORTANCE OF HANDLING SCRIPTURE WELL

the pledge out to you. And if he is a poor man, you shall not sleep in his pledge. You shall restore to him the pledge as the sun sets, that he may sleep in his cloak and bless you. (Deut. 24:10–15)

Such passages shed a strong light on how God expects his people to treat one another, particularly when one of them is in need. What they do not address, at least not automatically or in the same way, is the believer's obligation to the needy beyond the believing community. Why should such a distinction matter? Because we want to treat God's Word with integrity, letting it say what it says and not what we wish it to say. The simple fact is, the Old Testament was often careful to distinguish between those within the covenant community and those without, and God's directions for the two were not always the same (e.g., Deut. 14:21). Thus we do Scripture a disservice when we collapse the distinction as if it were irrelevant.

To discover God's intentions for Israel's relations to the non-Israelite poor, we do better to turn to those sections dealing with the treatment of aliens, foreigners, strangers, or sojourners (e.g., Ex. 22:21; 23:9). These texts speak more directly to the question of how insiders are to relate to those outside the believing community. Yet even here, as we noted in an earlier section, these legal stipulations had to do with nonbelievers who were resident within or passing through Israel's boundaries. They were thus hospitality laws, stipulating how visitors and outsiders within God's theocratic community were to be treated. They did not address the Israelite's social obligations to other societies beyond the covenant community's boundaries. On this subject the Old Testament is virtually silent.

Heightened Obligations. We must be careful not to absolutize this distinction. It's not as if our third and fourth circles of application, the covenant community and society at large, are hermetically sealed categories which have nothing to do with each other. Even those passages oriented expressly toward relationships within the believing community are not irrelevant to the world beyond. But neither can we simply draw a straight line from the one to the other, as if the distinction bears no significance. The Bible often emphasizes this distinction and calls believers to a *heightened obligation* to one another. Ignoring this point may lead to a trifecta of spiritual failure: of our Lord, of his Word, and of his people.

These pitfalls are not merely hypothetical. Once we have our antenna up, it is, unfortunately, not difficult to find examples of precisely this mistake. I recently heard a well-known Christian leader address a large gathering

> Let us do good to everyone, and especially to those who are of the household of faith.
> —Gal. 6:10

on the subject of the church's ministry to the needy. Every category of the world's needs—hunger, poverty, human trafficking, clean water, AIDS, political oppression, etc.—was vividly portrayed before the audience, and passages such as the above were repeatedly employed as motivation for the Christian's involvement in ameliorating those needs. But we heard not a word about the needs of suffering Christians around the world, much less those who are suffering expressly for Christ's sake. One would never have guessed from this presentation that believers bear a *heightened obligation* of care for their fellow Christians. The focus was entirely upon the world's needs in general. Thus were these powerful passages, shorn of their context, harnessed to make the speaker's point, but at the expense of allowing them to make their own.

At issue here, again, is how we use the Bible. The question is not whether Christians bear obligations to the needy beyond the boundaries of the church. I have already insisted that we do. Our point is a more focused one. It has to do with our commitment to treat Scripture with care, refusing to yank biblical passages from their context in order to enlist them into the service of our own arguments, however worthy.

If these Old Testament passages are to be deployed at all, they must be deployed in ways that first do full justice to their primary focus. From there we may be able to build legitimate (but also complex and, not seldom, controversial and far from self-evident[3]) interpretational linkages to the question of the broader needs of the world. But we will only discover those legitimate linkages by first handling these texts carefully, allowing them to be what they are instead of forcing them into some predetermined, decontextualized mold.

COUNTING THE REFERENCES

If the Old Testament law is particularly susceptible to misapplication in this discussion, one sometimes sees another, even broader practice that is equally problematic. In an attempt to energize Christians in their concern for the poor—again, among the worthiest of motives—it is not uncommon to hear the number of biblical references to the poor adduced as evidence for how much God truly cares for those who are suffering. This impressive figure, numbering in the many hundreds, is designed to demonstrate how important the poor are to the heart of God. Hence, the argument goes, they should be important to us as well.

Let there be no question that the needs of the poor and the vulnerable—"the sojourner, the fatherless, and the widow" (Deut. 27:19)—are important, perhaps we should say uniquely so, to God, and should therefore be important to us. "My whole being will exclaim, 'Who is like you, O Lord?' You rescue the poor from those too strong for them, the poor and needy from those who rob them" (Ps. 35:10 NIV). Yet this way of demonstrating God's concern—simply numbering the references in the Bible—is a particularly misleading way of making the case. It does a disservice to a wide range of biblical texts by glossing over their unique messages and bending them all to a single purpose, a purpose which may or may not reflect their true intent.

The point of citing this large conglomeration of references is not merely to prove that the subject of the poor is a common one in Scripture; that would be true enough but also unhelpfully ambiguous. The implication, rather, is that this collection of passages all make essentially the same point and can therefore be aggregated to emphasize a central conclusion: namely, that God has a special place in his heart (a preference) for a generic category of people called "the poor."

But just here is where this argument fails. These varied passages do not all say the same thing about the poor. In fact, there is no such general category in the Bible as "the poor." The Bible's references to the poor are far too nuanced and multidimensional for that; they simply cannot be stuffed into such a generic pot. We do a disservice to the complexity of what the Bible has to say about poor people even to suggest, directly or indirectly, that they can. Leveling out the Bible's many references to the poor as if they are all dealing with some general, undifferentiated category is a surefire prescription for missing what the Bible actually has to say on the subject.

Consider, for instance, the testimony of the book of Proverbs. As we have already seen, Proverbs calls us to serve the poor, those who are vulnerable or suffering unfairly. But this does not exhaust what Proverbs says about the poor. Sometimes, we are told, people are poor not because of oppression but because they are *slothful*:

> A slack hand causes poverty,
> but the hand of the diligent makes rich. (Prov. 10:4)

> In all toil there is profit,
> but mere talk tends only to poverty. (Prov. 14:23)

I passed by the field of a sluggard,
    by the vineyard of a man lacking sense,
and behold, it was all overgrown with thorns;
    the ground was covered with nettles,
    and its stone wall was broken down.
Then I saw and considered it;
    I looked and received instruction.
A little sleep, a little slumber,
    a little folding of the hands to rest,
and poverty will come upon you like a robber,
    and want like an armed man. (Prov. 24:30–34)

Whoever works his land will have plenty of bread,
    but he who follows worthless pursuits will
      have plenty of poverty. (Prov. 28:19)

Or because people are *self-indulgent*:

The drunkard and the glutton will come to poverty,
    and slumber will clothe them with
      rags. (Prov. 23:21)

Whoever loves pleasure will be a poor man;
    he who loves wine and oil will not
      be rich. (Prov. 21:17)

Or because they are *unteachable*:

Poverty and disgrace come to him
    who ignores instruction,
but whoever heeds reproof is honored. (Prov. 13:18)

Proverbs thus differentiates among several potential reasons for poverty. Poor people are apparently not all alike. Both the victim of oppression and the sluggard may be impoverished, but we fail them both if we collapse them into a single category called "the poor." What's worse: we do God's Word a disservice.

Drawing conclusions from the sheer number of references

to the poor in the Bible ignores the unique message of each of these actual references. It levels them out as if they are all saying the same thing. But of course, as the book of Proverbs alone demonstrates, they aren't. Both Judas Iscariot and Jesus refer to the poor in John 12:4–8, but neither reference would fit nicely into some general category. Each of the Bible's references to the poor must be treated with integrity, in its own context. It must be allowed to speak with its own voice. When we do that, we discover that the Bible's teaching about the poor is far richer and more nuanced than any general statistic could convey.

Our purpose in citing this proverbial counsel is not to justify dividing the needy into the so-called deserving poor and the undeserving poor and then concluding that we are obligated only to those who deserve our help. The fact is, even if we could discern who is truly deserving and who is not— which, being both sinful and fallible, we are usually unable to do—we bear an obligation to all people, because they are fellow image bearers of God, if nothing else. The counsel of Proverbs may help us make better judgments about what sort of help is most useful in given instances, but it does not relieve us of responsibility for helping even those whose poverty may be self-inflicted. Our point here has to do not with how to avoid helping the "undeserving" poor, but with how not to use the Bible.

TWO STRATEGIES

These considerations demonstrate how carefully the biblical text must be handled in our "word versus deed" discussion. In our desire to further various worthwhile social agendas, particularly those focused on the world's poor, we can all too easily descend into flagrant proof-texting, deploying decontextualized verses to buttress our arguments. Why does this happen? It may in part be because, when handled aright, we discover the Bible offers less explicit support to some parts of our argument than we might like. We want it to say more than it does.

We spoke earlier of five concentric circles of application: the personal, the family, the believing community, society in general, and the natural creation. As we noted then, advocates for social activism often wish to address the fourth circle, and increasingly the fifth. Human suffering, they stress, is not only the result of sinful individuals; it is the result of sinful social structures, structures that are sinful precisely because they are erected, maintained, and inhabited by sinful people so as to marginalize and oppress the weak and disadvantaged. Thus God's people are called to challenge these societal structures and seek to correct them. It is one of the primary callings of the church, they want to argue, to seek out the needy beyond the believing community in order to alleviate human suffering.

The difficulty is, as we previously emphasized, if we wish to enlist the Bible in such an argument, we are hard-pressed to find biblical passages that *in any direct way* specify and advocate such a calling. Passages addressing the first three circles are not just present in the Bible; they are ubiquitous and explicit. But the same cannot be said for the fourth (and fifth) circles. The Old Testament is rife with concern for issues of justice and mercy within the covenant community, but nowhere do we find the Israelites being instructed to challenge the unjust social structures of the surrounding peoples. The Roman Empire of the New Testament era was the epitome of an unjust society, but nowhere do Jesus or his apostles argue, in any direct way, that challenging these structures is the task of the church.[4] On the contrary, about the only thing Jesus ever taught about the believer's relationship to Rome was, "Render to Caesar the things that are Caesar's"

(Matt. 22:21). The apostle Paul was echoing Jesus's point and expanding on it when he said:

> Let every person be subject to the governing authorities. For there is no authority except from God, and those that exist have been instituted by God. Therefore whoever resists the authorities resists what God has appointed, and those who resist will incur judgment. For rulers are not a terror to good conduct, but to bad. Would you have no fear of the one who is in authority? Then do what is good, and you will receive his approval, for he is God's servant for your good. But if you do wrong, be afraid, for he does not bear the sword in vain. For he is the servant of God, an avenger who carries out God's wrath on the wrongdoer. Therefore one must be in subjection, not only to avoid God's wrath but also for the sake of conscience. For because of this you also pay taxes, for the authorities are ministers of God, attending to this very thing. Pay to all what is owed to them: taxes to whom taxes are owed, revenue to whom revenue is owed, respect to whom respect is owed, honor to whom honor is owed. (Rom. 13:1–7)

The simple fact is that while the New Testament has a great deal to say about the first three circles of application, it has relatively little to say about the fourth and fifth. And what it does say scarcely constitutes a prophetic challenge. The direct apostolic instructions actually sound rather tame:

> First of all, then, I urge that supplications, prayers, intercessions, and thanksgivings be made for all people, for kings and all who are in high positions, that we may lead a peaceful and quiet life, godly and dignified in every way. This is good, and it is pleasing in the sight of God our Savior, who desires all people to be saved and to come to the knowledge of the truth. (1 Tim. 2:1–4)

So what is a social activist who wants to enlist the authority of the Bible to do? Two strategies are available. The illegitimate one, as we have seen (and will see again in the next chapter), is to decontextualize the biblical passages dealing with the third circle, the believing community, transforming them into proof-texts that can be pressed into the service of the fourth circle, society at large. Does the passage speak of the poor, of mercy, of justice? Never mind that it's addressing poverty, mercy, and justice within the believing community; ignore this inconvenient fact and deploy the passage for the broader cause. Unfortunately, this is the strategy we see employed far too often in the "word versus deed" discussion.

A more legitimate strategy, by contrast, requires more care and hard work. The Bible can indeed be enlisted on the side of caring for human needs beyond the believing community and addressing the sinful social structures of our day. But not via proof-texting. A more justifiable strategy requires careful extrapolation from what the Bible actually *does* say to the needs of our contemporary, globalized world. Such an approach requires thoughtful exegetical, hermeneutical, and theological reasoning to build its case, reasoning that must be made explicit rather than merely assumed. Only in this way can its linkages be tested and validated.

In previous chapters we examined five useful lines of biblical thought: godly wisdom, neighbor love, kingdom building, adorning the gospel, and stewardship of the creation. All of these abstract themes are the outworking of a still higher insight focused on the nature of God and his general will for creation: he is a God of love, mercy, and justice who is redeeming the entire created order, and he wills humans to emulate him in all of their relationships. Our challenge is to work our way down the ladder as we attempt to tease out what such emulation requires at ground level.

The difficulty with this strategy, of course, is that, as noted above, such moves down the ladder inevitably introduce elements of uncertainty and even controversy. Every such move requires presuppositions others may question; it involves building a structure of thought, not all of which may be equally compelling. And the more specific we are, the more evident this problem becomes. Blind spots work their magic so that a concern for individual issues, for example, may eclipse corporate concerns, or vice versa. The entire process lies vulnerable to our human frailty. Yet it has this to be said for it. However this interpretational move down the ladder is managed, well or poorly, those who attempt it demonstrate at least this virtue: they are refusing to make their biblical case on the basis of a tissue of decontextualized proof-texts.

CHAPTER THIRTEEN

THREE KEY PASSAGES

Make a mistake in the interpretation of one of Shakespeare's plays, falsely scan a piece of Spenserian verse, and there is unlikely to be an entailment of eternal consequences; but we cannot lightly accept a similar laxity in the interpretation of Scripture. We are dealing with God's thoughts.

—D. A. Carson

Whenever the Bible is brought to bear on the "word versus deed" question, there are three passages that are almost certain to be cited. They show up regularly in this discourse and, because they are all pertinent to the subject, they are often allowed to exert a strong influence on the discussion's conclusions. But alas, these passages do not always fare well in the hands of their interpreters. They are often mishandled, and therefore misrepresented, by those who cite them most enthusiastically. All three passages deserve better care.

JEREMIAH 29:4–7

This often-cited passage demonstrates how easily and commonly Bible verses are decontextualized in order to press them into foreign service. Consider the following background to Jeremiah 29.

The Jewish prophets repeatedly warned the people of Judah that unless they relinquished their idolatry and returned to the Lord, they would be disciplined. But they refused to obey, so the Lord sent Jeremiah with this message: "Because you have not obeyed my words, behold, I will send for all the tribes of the north, declares the Lord, and for Nebuchadnezzar the king of Babylon, my servant, and I will bring them against this land and its inhabitants" (Jer. 25:8–9). Thus it was that, as an unwitting instrument of God, Babylon's Nebuchadnezzar besieged Jerusalem and carted the Jews off to the very cradle of idolatry for an extended period of exile.

Later, after the exiles had arrived in Babylon, God sent them a second word through Jeremiah. This message came in the form of a letter:

> Thus says the Lord of hosts, the God of Israel, to all the exiles whom I have sent into exile from Jerusalem to Babylon: Build houses and live in them; plant gardens and eat their produce. Take wives and have sons and daughters; take wives for your sons, and give your daughters in marriage, that they may bear sons and daughters; multiply there, and do not decrease. But seek the welfare of the city where I have sent you into exile, and pray to the Lord on its behalf, for in its welfare you will find your welfare. (Jer. 29:4–7)

These verses are commonly cited as a rationale for the church's social obligations to the world at large. Like those exiles in Babylon, it is said, we too are "sojourners and exiles" in the world (1 Pet. 2:11). And like them, God calls us to seek the welfare of the place of our sojourn. He commissions his people to be about the business of serving and improving society at large in the communities in which they live.

A Misguided Conclusion. The problem is that drawing this conclusion from Jeremiah 29 distorts the passage and misrepresents God's explicitly stated intent. If we allow these verses their own voice, set in their own context, we discover that the motive for God's instruction to seek "the welfare of the city" had little to do with improving things for the Babylonians.

The point of God's word through Jeremiah was to instruct the exiles in how to make the best of their disciplinary experience.

God was, for the time being, using Babylon as an instrument to chastise his own people. Moreover, he wanted them to understand, contrary to the false prophets (cf. Jer. 27:9; 29:28), that their captivity in Babylon would not be merely a brief dislocation: "Your exile will be long" (Jer. 29:28), he instructed them; indeed, it would last for seventy years (Jer. 25:10–11; 29:10). Thus the exiles were not to view themselves as temporary refugees. They were now inhabitants who must patiently settle down and make a life for themselves. They were to build houses and live in them; plant gardens and eat their produce; they were to marry and grow families and increase in number.[1]

It was in this vein, then, that they were to "seek the welfare of the city" where God had placed them. Instead of hunkering down in refugee camps or perhaps resisting or attempting to subvert their captors from within, the exiles were to acknowledge God's purposes for their exile and reconcile themselves (see Jer. 21:9) to the fact that they were now Babylonian residents. Thus they should pray not for God's judgment on their captors but for God's mercy and patience toward Babylon, "for in its welfare you will find your welfare."

The focus of this passage is thus not the flourishing of Babylon but the well-being of God's people. To conclude otherwise is to mistake the means for an end. Even in their time of chastening, God's covenant people were the object of his love. The sense of relief expressed in Jeremiah 29:10–14, which speaks of the end of the exile and the Israelites' return to Jerusalem, is not merely the people's but the Lord's. Verses 4–7 may therefore be enlisted as further evidence of God's special care for his own, but citing it as an indication of God's concern for the well-being of Babylon stretches the point beyond what the passage will bear.

Let it be clearly said that believers are indeed to serve the common good in their communities and bless that part of the world where God has placed them. But the question before us is, should we be using Jeremiah 29 to make this point? Here's the puzzle: can it be, given the uniform testimony of Scripture to the contrary, that God was interested in the flourishing of the Babylonians?

> As I live, declares the Lord GOD, I have no pleasure in the death of the wicked, but that the wicked turn from his way and live.
>
> —Ezek. 33:11

If that flourishing involved coming to know him, the answer may well be yes. Consider the city of Nineveh. Its wickedness was an affront to God (Jonah 1:2). Yet, according to Jonah, the Lord is "a gracious God and merciful, slow to anger and abounding in steadfast love, and relenting from disaster" (4:2). Thus he commissioned Jonah to take a message of repentance to the Ninevites so that they might escape his judgment. When Jonah was annoyed that the plan actually worked, God said to him, "Should not I pity Nineveh, that great city, in which there are more than 120,000 persons who do not know their right hand from their left, and also much cattle?" (vv. 10–11; see also Ezek. 18:23; 33:10–11). God was clearly concerned for the Ninevites, but it was not for their general well-being. It was that they might come to know him as their God, apart from which they would experience only calamity.

In the same way we may assume that God was concerned for the people of Babylon. But his concern was not for their cultural welfare. There is nothing in Jeremiah 29 to suggest that God was interested in their domestic flourishing. Indeed, there can be no genuine human flourishing ("never seek their peace or prosperity," Ezra 9:12; see also Deut. 23:6) apart from Jehovah (Num. 6:24–26), the one true God whom the

Babylonians had long repudiated. As C. S. Lewis put it, "God cannot give us a happiness and peace apart from Himself, because it is not there. There is no such thing."[2]

Just as God could temporarily use Babylon to discipline his people,[3] so he could for a time prosper the Babylonians to bless his people. But that temporary prosperity was always a means to an end, not an end in itself. If we are to take God at his word, by the time of Jeremiah's letter to the exiles his purposes for Babylon were already determined, and they had nothing to do with Babylon's flourishing. The notion that Jeremiah 29:4–7 is teaching that God wished Babylon well is contravened by the explicit testimony of God himself.

To the faithful exiles (the "good figs" of Jeremiah 24) God had said: "When seventy years are completed for Babylon, I will visit you, and I will fulfill to you my promise [see Jer. 24:5–7] and bring you back to this place. For I know the plans I have for you, declares the LORD, plans for welfare and not for evil, to give you a future and a hope" (Jer. 29:10–11). But his equally certain plans for Babylon were dramatically different:

> Then after seventy years are completed, I will punish the king of Babylon and that nation, the land of the Chaldeans, for their iniquity, declares the LORD, making the land an everlasting waste. I will bring upon that land all the words that I have uttered against it, everything written in this book [see Jeremiah 50–51], which Jeremiah prophesied against all the nations. For many nations and great kings shall make slaves even of them, and I will recompense them according to their deeds and the work of their hands. (Jer. 25:12–14; see also Hab. 1:6; 2:6–20)

God's intent for Babylon was not for its flourishing. Babylon was set for destruction before the exiles ever arrived. To cite one decontextualized verse in Jeremiah 29 as evidence that God wished Babylon well, despite its historic and rampant idolatry (Jer. 50:38), its in-your-face desecration of God's temple in Jerusalem (Jer. 50:28; 51:11; see also 52:12–23; Dan. 1:1–2), its ultimate "iniquity" in taking God's people captive (Jer. 50:11)—and most importantly, despite God's clearly and forcefully expressed purposes to the contrary (e.g., Jer. 50:45; 51:11–12, 29)—badly distorts the point of this important passage. A more instructive insight into what God was saying to the exiles in Jeremiah 29:4–7 may be the parallel instructions Paul would one day give first-century Christians with regard to Rome:

> I urge, then, first of all, that requests, prayers, intercession and thanksgiving be made for everyone—for kings and all those in authority, that we may live peaceful and quiet lives in all godliness and holiness. (1 Tim. 2:1–2 NIV)

Should believers pray for the community where God has placed them, serving the people there in Christ's name while modeling human flourishing in their midst? Absolutely. This is part of what it means to be the salt and light Christ calls his church to be. There are numerous passages in the Bible that urge us in precisely this direction. But Jeremiah 29:4–7 should not be numbered among them.

LUKE 4:16–21

This passage is significant because it records Jesus's own summary of his purpose in coming. His public ministry was in full swing, but he had not yet turned toward Jerusalem and what awaited him there; he was still early in the process of making himself known. Thus, Luke tells us, he came "in the power of the Spirit to Galilee, and a report about him went out through all the surrounding country. And he taught in their synagogues, being glorified by all" (Luke 4:14–15). Eventually Jesus arrived in the village of Nazareth "where he had been brought up. And as was his custom, he went to the synagogue on the Sabbath day" (vv. 16–17). There he stood up to read:

> The scroll of the prophet Isaiah was given to him. He unrolled the scroll and found the place where it was written, "The Spirit of the Lord is upon me, because he has anointed me to proclaim good news to the poor. He has sent me to proclaim liberty to the captives and recovering of sight to the blind, to set at liberty those who are oppressed, to proclaim the year of the Lord's favor." And he rolled up the scroll and gave it back to the attendant and sat down. And the eyes of all in the synagogue were fixed on him. And he began to say to them, "Today this Scripture has been fulfilled in your hearing." (vv. 17–21)

The words Jesus quoted here were drawn largely from Isaiah 61; he used this passage to announce himself to the people of Nazareth as the promised Servant of Jehovah. It was a wonderfully dramatic moment. In this historically significant but nonetheless out-of-the-way place, Jesus was announcing his true identity to those among whom he had grown up. How startling it must have been for his listeners to hear Jesus say of this classic passage, "Today this Scripture has been fulfilled in your hearing."

Luke 4 is commonly offered up as marching orders for the church. Here Jesus announces the special focus of his kingdom, it is said. His kingdom represents good news for the poor, freedom for the prisoners, sight for the blind, and release for those who are oppressed. This is what Jesus's ministry was about, and if we claim to be doing the business of his kingdom, this is what we must be about. We too must care for the poor, heal the sick, visit the prisoners, and bring justice to the oppressed. This sort of social activism is what Jesus says the kingdom of God is about.

Such conclusions, argued on the basis of this particular passage, are fairly common. But they are also problematic.

We should not call into question the notion that God's people are to be involved in caring for the poor and healing the sick and releasing the oppressed. Our issue here is, once again, a more pointed one: should we be making this point *from this particular passage*?

Let us say, perhaps. But if so, this much is certain. The connections between what Jesus declared in Nazareth and general conclusions about the church's sociopolitical agenda in the society at large require much more attention than the facile treatment they popularly receive. What will not do, if we are to treat this key passage with the care it deserves, is jumping immediately from Jesus's references to the poor, the blind, the captives, and the oppressed in Luke 4 to a social agenda in our contemporary secular setting. A more careful examination of this passage demonstrates that any such leaps require a good deal of qualification.

We cannot attempt a full-scale exegetical treatment of Isaiah 61 and Luke 4, but here are some of the issues that should warn us away from simplistic treatments of this important text.

First, this is an exceptionally complicated passage to exegete faithfully. It represents an intricate blend of Isaiah's original multilevel message to his audience, Jesus's use of Isaiah's message as a vehicle for his own message to a different audience, and Luke's point in recording it all for a still different audience. Such multidimensional passages are very poor candidates for simplistic applications.

Second, we must not leapfrog the essential theocratic setting of this passage. The promises of Isaiah 60 and 61 are specifically focused on "those who mourn in Zion—to give them a beautiful headdress instead of ashes, the oil of gladness instead of mourning, the garment of praise instead of a faint spirit" (61:3). Jesus was an Israelite, speaking to an Israelite audience, in an Israelite setting, from the Israelite

Scriptures, identifying himself as the promised completion of Israel's story and eschatological solution to Israel's anguish. No application that fails to do justice to this crucial context can hope to be faithful to the passage.

Third, moving immediately to broad sociopolitical applications from this passage will almost certainly underplay its spiritual dimension. We can see this by considering the passage itself.

The "poor" to whom the gospel is such good news in this passage, for both Isaiah and Jesus, were not merely any who are materially lacking; they were members of the people of God who, because of their poverty, were especially open and responsive to God. They were those

> It is well known that "the poor" in the Old Testament were not just the needy but the pious whose hope and trust were in God.
> —John Stott

who met God's own definition of the one he esteems: "He who is humble and contrite in spirit and trembles at my word" (Isa. 66:2). For Jesus, the poor are those who suffer precisely because they demonstrate these characteristics. They are, so to speak, the *righteous* poor, those who are "poor in spirit" (Matt. 5:3), those who "hunger and thirst for righteousness" (v. 6) and are "pure in heart" (v. 8). Their poverty is related to their being "persecuted because of righteousness" on account of their relationship to Jesus (vv. 10–11 NIV). He likens them to the very prophets of old who likewise suffered for their faithfulness:

> Blessed are you who are poor, for yours is the kingdom of God. Blessed are you who are hungry now, for you shall be satisfied. Blessed are you who weep now, for you shall laugh. Blessed are you when people hate you and when they exclude you and revile you and spurn your name as evil, *on account of the Son of Man*! Rejoice in that day, and leap for

joy, for behold, your reward is great in heaven; for so their fathers did to the prophets. (Luke 6:20–23)

The promise of these beatitudes, and of Luke 4, is not to just anyone who is impoverished. The poverty Jesus had in mind had strong spiritual overtones. His was not a guarantee of release from material lack in this life; Jesus's promise was to those who are trusting God. It was a promise that while they may be poor and hungry and sorrowful and hated now, it will not always be so. One day through him the tables will be turned and great will be their reward in heaven. What Jesus was announcing in the synagogue in Nazareth was the dawn of that eschatological day.

Similarly, the "captives" in this passage are not just anyone clapped into prison. There were spiritual dimensions to their imprisonment. In Isaiah they are captives to the abuse of the nations due to their sin and rebellion (Isaiah 58–59). But the promise of the Lord to them through Isaiah was that it would not always be so:

> The sons of those who afflicted you
>   shall come bending low to you,
> and all who despised you
>   shall bow down at your feet;
> they shall call you the City of the Lord,
>   the Zion of the Holy One of Israel.
> Whereas you have been forsaken and hated,
>   with no one passing through,
> I will make you majestic forever,
>   a joy from age to age. (60:14–15)

Jesus's use of Isaiah's reference to captives thus carried strong spiritual overtones. The promised release was related to the eschatological day that Jesus, the Isaiahic Servant of Jehovah, was now inaugurating. Ultimately the captives would be free in every sense of the term, but in the meantime the release Jesus was promising was not physical; it was a release from a far more consequential slavery for all who would follow him: "Truly, truly, I say to you, everyone who practices sin is a slave to sin. The slave does not remain in the house forever; the son remains forever. So if the Son sets you free, you will be free indeed" (John 8:34–36).

> It is true that in the Old Testament *shalom* . . . often indicates political and material well-being. But can it be maintained, as serious biblical exegesis, that the New Testament authors present Jesus Christ as winning this kind of peace and as bestowing it on society as a whole? . . . *[S]halom* is the blessing the Messiah brings to his people.
>
> —John Stott

In the same way, the reference to giving sight to the blind carried inevitable spiritual overtones. Blindness and sight, darkness and light, are common spiritual motifs in the ministry of Jesus. Jesus healed the blind, but those physical healings, as with all of his miracles, were never self-contained acts of mercy. They were certainly marvelous acts of mercy, but they were always more: signs pointing to something beyond. Jesus's promise of bringing sight to the blind was a profoundly spiritual promise.

And "the year of the Lord's favor"? Leviticus 25 speaks of Israel's ancient year of Jubilee. Every fiftieth year in Israel trumpets would sound liberty throughout the land. Fields were to lie fallow, people were returned to their own land, debts were forgiven, and slaves set free. Jubilee was a gracious provision for Israel's communal life, but ultimately it was a picture of the spaciousness of God's forgiveness and the spiritual liberation that came with it. In citing this

THE IMPORTANCE OF HANDLING SCRIPTURE WELL

reference in Isaiah, it certainly was not the literal Jubilee Jesus was announcing. Jesus was inaugurating the eschatological Jubilee, the sweeping physical and spiritual liberation the ancient Jubilee pointed toward.

Finally, any application of Luke 4 to our contemporary setting must keep front and center the most critical point of all; namely, that there is no kingdom apart from the King.

This passage is too often reduced by advocates to a sociopolitical agenda: the kingdom of God, it is said, is about serving the poor, reaching out to the prisoners, healing the blind, and bringing release to the oppressed. But such a reductionist treatment badly distorts the point of the passage. The kingdom of God is not about any of these things *in themselves*. The kingdom of God is first and foremost about the King; it's about *Jesus* as the centerpiece of each of these things. Jesus himself—who he is, what he has done, what he is doing, what he will do—*is* the ultimate good news for which the poor are so desperate.

No treatment of Luke 4 that settles for a sociopolitical agenda can thus do justice to what Jesus was announcing in this crucial passage. The simple fact is that Jesus does not always release the poor from material poverty, or free prisoners from their jail cells, or heal physical blindness, or remove oppression, even for those who follow him. So what was Jesus offering? He was offering himself, and the ultimate promise of each of these things in the eschatological fulfillment of his kingdom. He is the one who brings genuine liberation to the captive; he is the one who can truly set the prisoner free; he is the one who brings ultimate release to the oppressed; he is the one who gives spiritual sight. These are the true fruits of the kingdom.

We may well conclude from other passages of the Bible that we are to serve God today by working to alleviate social, political and economic ills in the world at large. But we do Luke 4 a disservice when, by denuding it of its spiritual, eschatological, Christocentric dimensions, we reduce it to a de-Christianized social agenda. The marching orders we find in this important passage are focused first and foremost not on improving society per se but on offering Jesus and his kingdom promises to all who will receive them. He is the fulfillment of Isaiah 61. Without him as King, there can be no kingdom.

MATTHEW 25:31–46

This third example of scriptural mishandling in the "word versus deed" discussion is perhaps the most common, and because of that probably the most egregious. In this famous passage Jesus gives his account of that great climactic scene:

> When the Son of Man comes in his glory, and all the angels with him, then he will sit on his glorious throne. Before him will be gathered all the nations, and he will separate people one from another as a shepherd separates the sheep from the goats. And he will place the sheep on his right, but the goats on the left. (Matt. 25:31–33)

On what basis will the King choose between the sheep and goats? Jesus portrays both groups as surprised by the answer. To the sheep he says:

> Come, you who are blessed by my Father, inherit the kingdom prepared for you from the foundation of the world. For I was hungry and you gave me food, I was thirsty and you gave me drink, I was a stranger and you welcomed me, I was naked and you clothed me, I was sick and you visited me, I was in prison and you came to me. (vv. 34–36)

Puzzled by this explanation, the righteous protest: "Lord, when did we do these things to you?" (see vv. 37–38). Jesus answers, in these well-known words, "Truly, I say to you, as you did it to one of the least of these my brothers, you did it to me" (v. 40). The passage then concludes with a similar but opposite word to the goats: "Truly, I say to you, as you did not do it to one of the least of these, you did not do it to me" (v. 45).

This famous passage is consistently treated as if Jesus is speaking here in some generalized way about the poor. Whenever we minister to a poor person, it is said, we are in fact ministering to Jesus. When we give food to the hungry, we are giving it to Jesus; when we give water to the parched, we are giving it to Jesus; when we clothe that naked person, we are clothing Jesus; when we visit the prisoner, we are visiting Jesus; when we show hospitality to a needy stranger, we are showing hospitality to Jesus. Jesus so identified with the poor of the world, it is claimed, that he comes to us embodied in the one who is suffering, such that whatever we do for that needy person we are doing for him. For those who truly love Jesus, this is offered as, and in fact becomes, a powerful motive for selfless deeds of compassion and justice.

The difficulty is that this is not what this passage, or any other passage of the Bible, is teaching. Such a bold claim may startle readers who have heard Matthew 25 used this way so often they take it for granted. But a careful inspection of this important text demonstrates that it is teaching something rather more particular.

The key to understanding what Jesus is teaching in Matthew 25 lies in Jesus's explanation to both those who had and those who had not ministered to him: "Truly, I say to you, as you did it to one of the least of these my brothers, you did it to me"; and, "Truly, I say to you, as you did not do it to one of the least of these, you did not do it to me" (vv. 40, 45). Who are "the least of these my brothers"? Is Jesus referring here to any and all needy people, or to a more specific group? How we answer this question will dictate what we understand Jesus to be teaching in this important passage.

Given how often this text is mishandled, one might conclude that this is a difficult interpretive puzzle to solve. In fact, it isn't. All we require is a modicum of attention to the biblical and theological context for Jesus's statements. The following series of six straightforward, unobjectionable affirmations provides that context. Rather than offering my own interpretive comments, I have buttressed these six affirmations with extensive biblical quotations so as to allow the Scriptures to speak for themselves.

SIX ASSERTIONS

1) The apostle Paul taught that believers constitute the extended body of Christ.

> For as in one body we have many members, and the members do not all have the same function, so *we, though many, are one body in Christ*, and individually members one of another. (Rom. 12:4–5)

> For just as the body is one and has many members, and all the members of the body, though many, are one body, *so it is with Christ*. For in one Spirit we were all baptized into one body—Jews or Greeks, slaves or free—and all were made to drink of one Spirit. For the body does not consist of one member but of many. . . . Now *you are the body of Christ and individually members of it*. (1 Cor. 12:12–14, 27)

> And he gave the apostles, the prophets, the evangelists, the shepherds and teachers, to equip the saints for the work of ministry, for building up *the body of Christ*, until we all attain to the unity of the faith and of the knowledge of the Son of God, to mature manhood, to the measure of the stature of the fullness of Christ. (Eph. 4:11–13)

> Wives, submit to your own husbands, as to the Lord. For the husband is the head of the wife even as Christ *is the head of the church, his body*, and is himself its Savior. (Eph. 5:22–23)

2) Paul gained his first insight into this concept of believers as the embodiment of Christ from Jesus himself.

> But Saul, still breathing threats and murder against *the disciples of the Lord*, went to the high priest and asked him for letters to the synagogues at Damascus, so that if he found any belonging to the Way, men or women, he might bring them bound to Jerusalem. Now as he went on his way, he approached Damascus, and suddenly a light from heaven shone around him. And falling to the ground he heard a voice saying to him, "Saul, Saul, *why are you persecuting me?*" And he said, "Who are you, Lord?" And he said, "*I am Jesus, whom you are persecuting.*" (Acts 9:1–5)

3) Jesus taught that his faithful followers, his body, would suffer for his name's sake.

> Blessed are those who are persecuted for righteousness' sake, for theirs is the kingdom of heaven. Blessed are you when others revile you and persecute you and utter all kinds of evil against you falsely *on my account*. Rejoice and be glad, for your reward is great in heaven, for so they persecuted the prophets who were before you. (Matt. 5:10–12)

> Behold, I am sending you out as sheep in the midst of wolves, so be wise as serpents and innocent as doves. Beware of men, for they will deliver you over to courts and flog you in their synagogues, and you will be dragged before governors and kings *for my sake*, to bear witness before them and the Gentiles. When they deliver you over, do not be anxious how you are to speak or what you are to say, for what you are to say will be given to you in that hour. For it is not you who speak, but the Spirit of your Father speaking through you. Brother will deliver brother over to death, and the father his child, and children will rise against parents and have them put to death, and you will be hated by all *for my name's sake*. But the one who endures to the end will be saved. When they persecute you in one town, flee to the next, for truly, I say to you, you will not have gone through all the towns of Israel before the Son of Man comes. A disciple is not above

his teacher, nor a servant above his master. *It is enough for the disciple to be like his teacher, and the servant like his master. If they have called the master of the house Beelzebul, how much more will they malign those of his household.* So have no fear of them, for nothing is covered that will not be revealed, or hidden that will not be known. What I tell you in the dark, say in the light, and what you hear whispered, proclaim on the housetops. And do not fear those who kill the body but cannot kill the soul. Rather fear him who can destroy both soul and body in hell. (Matt. 10:16–28)

And he lifted up his eyes on his disciples, and said: "Blessed are you who are poor, for yours is the kingdom of God. Blessed are you who are hungry now, for you shall be satisfied. Blessed are you who weep now, for you shall laugh. Blessed are you when people hate you and when they exclude you and revile you and spurn your name as evil, *on account of the Son of Man*! Rejoice in that day, and leap for joy, for behold, your reward is great in heaven; for so their fathers did to the prophets." (Luke 6:20–23)

But before all this they will lay their hands on you and persecute you, delivering you up to the synagogues and prisons, and you will be brought before kings and governors *for my name's sake*. (Luke 21:12)

If the world hates you, know that it has hated me before it hated you. If you were of the world, the world would love you as its own; but because you are not of the world, but I chose you out of the world, therefore the world hates you. Remember the word that I said to you: "A servant is not greater than his master." If they persecuted me, they will also persecute you. If they kept my word, they will also keep yours. But all these things they will do to you *on account of my name,* because they do not know him who sent me. (John 15:18–21)

4) Thus Christ's apostles taught the same thing; namely, that believers would suffer for Jesus's sake.

Bless those who *persecute you*; bless and do not curse them. (Rom. 12:14)

. . . that I may know him and the power of his resurrection, and may *share his sufferings*, becoming like him in his death, that by any means possible I may attain the resurrection from the dead. (Phil. 3:10–11)

For you, brothers, became imitators of the churches of God in Christ Jesus that are in Judea. For you *suffered the same things* from your own countrymen as they did from the Jews. (1 Thess. 2:14)

Therefore we ourselves boast about you in the churches of God for your steadfastness and faith in *all your persecutions and in the afflictions that you are enduring.* (2 Thess. 1:4)

Therefore do not be ashamed of the testimony about our Lord, nor of me his prisoner, but *share in suffering for the gospel* by the power of God. (2 Tim. 1:8)

Indeed, all who desire to live a godly life in Christ Jesus *will be persecuted.* (2 Tim. 3:12)

But recall the former days when, after you were enlightened, you *endured a hard struggle with sufferings*, sometimes being publicly *exposed to reproach and affliction*, and sometimes being partners with those so treated. For you had compassion on those in prison, and you joyfully accepted the *plundering of your property*, since you knew that you yourselves had a better possession and an abiding one. (Heb. 10:32–34)

And what more shall I say? For time would fail me to tell of Gideon, Barak, Samson, Jephthah, of David and Samuel and the prophets—who through faith conquered kingdoms, enforced justice, obtained promises, stopped the mouths of lions, quenched the power of fire, escaped the edge of the sword, were made strong out of weakness, became mighty in war, put foreign armies to flight. Women received back their dead by resurrection. Some were *tortured*, refusing to accept release, so that they might rise again to a better life. Others *suffered mocking and flogging, and even chains and imprisonment. They were stoned, they were sawn in two, they were killed with the sword. They went about in skins of sheep and goats, destitute, afflicted, mistreated—of whom the world was not worthy—wandering about in deserts and mountains, and in dens and caves of the earth.* (Heb. 11:32–38)

For what credit is it if, when you sin and are beaten for it, you endure? But if *when you do good and suffer for it* you endure, this is a gracious thing in the sight of God. For *to this you have been called*, because Christ also suffered for you, leaving you an example, so that you might follow in his steps. (1 Pet. 2:20–21)

Beloved, do not be surprised at the *fiery trial* when it comes upon you to test you, *as though something strange were happening to you*. But rejoice insofar as you *share Christ's sufferings*, that you may also rejoice and be glad when his glory is revealed. If you are *insulted for the name of Christ*, you are blessed, because the Spirit of glory and of God rests upon you. But let none of you suffer as a murderer or a thief or an evildoer or as a meddler. Yet if anyone *suffers as a Christian*, let him not be ashamed, but let him glorify God in that name. (1 Pet. 4:12–16)

Resist him, firm in your faith, knowing that *the same kinds of suffering are being experienced by your brotherhood throughout the world*. And after you have *suffered a little while*, the God of all grace, who has called you to his eternal glory in Christ, will himself restore, confirm, strengthen, and establish you. (1 Pet. 5:9–10)

I, John, your brother and *partner in the tribulation and the kingdom and the patient endurance that are in Jesus*, was on the island called Patmos *on account of the word of God and the testimony of Jesus*. (Rev. 1:9)

5) This concept of Christians, the extended body of Christ, suffering for Jesus's sake carries implications about the care

believers owe one another; namely, it means that Christians have a special obligation to other believers who are suffering, especially when they are suffering for their faith in Jesus.

> For truly, I say to you, whoever *gives you a cup of water to drink because you belong to Christ* will by no means lose his reward. Whoever causes *one of these little ones who believe in me* to sin, it would be better for him if a great millstone were hung around his neck and he were thrown into the sea. (Mark 9:41–42; see also Luke 17:1)

> And *all who believed* were together and had all things in common. And they were selling their possessions and belongings and *distributing the proceeds to all, as any had need.* (Acts 2:44–45)

> *Love one another with brotherly affection.* Outdo one another in showing honor. Do not be slothful in zeal, be fervent in spirit, serve the Lord. Rejoice in hope, be patient in tribulation, be constant in prayer. *Contribute to the needs of the saints and seek to show hospitality.* (Rom. 12:10–13)

> At present, however, I am going to Jerusalem *bringing aid to the saints.* For Macedonia and Achaia have been pleased to make some *contribution for the poor among the saints* at Jerusalem. (Rom. 15:25–26; see also 2 Cor. 9:1, 12)

> For just as the body is one and has many members, and all the members of the body, though many, are one body, *so it is with Christ.* For in one Spirit we were *all baptized into one body*— Jews or Greeks, slaves or free—and all were made to drink of one Spirit. For the body does not consist of one member but of many. . . . But God has so composed the body, giving greater honor to the part that lacked it, that there may be no division in the body, but that the members may *have the same care for one another. If one member suffers, all suffer together*; if one member is honored, all rejoice together. Now *you are the body of Christ and individually members of it.* (1 Cor. 12:12–27)

On the contrary, when they saw that I had been entrusted with the gospel to the uncircumcised, just as Peter had been entrusted with the gospel to the circumcised (for he who worked through Peter for his apostolic ministry to the circumcised worked also through me for mine to the Gentiles), and when James and Cephas and John, who seemed to be pillars, perceived the grace that was given to me, they gave the right hand of fellowship to Barnabas and me, that we should go to the Gentiles and they to the circumcised. Only, they asked us to *remember the poor*, the very thing I was eager to do. (Gal. 2:7–10; see also Acts 11:29–30; 24:17)

So then, as we have opportunity, let us do good to everyone, and *especially to those who are of the household of faith.* (Gal. 6:10)

You are aware that all who are in Asia turned away from me, among whom are Phygelus and Hermogenes. May the Lord grant mercy to the household of Onesiphorus, for he *often refreshed me and was not ashamed of my chains*, but when he arrived in Rome he *searched for me earnestly and found me*—may the Lord grant him to find mercy from the Lord on that Day!—and you well know *all the service he rendered at Ephesus.* (2 Tim. 1:15–18)

For God is not unjust so as to overlook your work and the *love that you have shown for his name in serving the saints, as you still do.* (Heb. 6:10)

Remember those who are in prison, *as though in prison with them, and those who are mistreated, since you also are in the body.* (Heb. 13:3)

Honor everyone. *Love the brotherhood.* Fear God. Honor the emperor. (1 Pet. 2:17)

By this we know love, that he laid down his life for us, and *we ought to lay down our lives for the brothers.* But if anyone has the world's goods and *sees his brother in need*, yet closes his heart against him, how does God's love abide in him? (1 John 3:16–17)

Beloved, it is a faithful thing you do in all your efforts *for these brothers, strangers as they are, who testified to your love before the church.* You will do well to *send them on their journey in a manner worthy of God.* For they have gone out for the sake of the name, accepting nothing from the Gentiles. Therefore *we ought to support people like these,* that we may be fellow workers for the truth. (3 John 5–8)

6) The concept of believers as the embodiment of Jesus also means that, just as in persecuting Christ's followers Saul of Tarsus was persecuting Jesus himself, so also in serving Christ's followers we are serving Jesus himself.

Whoever receives you receives me, and whoever receives me receives him who sent me. The one who *receives a prophet because he is a prophet* will receive a prophet's reward, and the one who *receives a righteous person because he is a righteous person* will receive a righteous person's reward. And whoever gives *one of these little ones even a cup of cold water because he is a disciple,* truly, I say to you, he will by no means lose his reward. (Matt. 10:40–42; see also Mark 9:37)

And calling to him a child, he put him in the midst of them and said, "Truly, I say to you, unless you turn and *become like children,* you will never enter the kingdom of heaven. Whoever humbles himself like this child is the greatest in the kingdom of heaven. *Whoever receives one such child in my name* receives me, but whoever causes *one of these little ones who believe in me* [cf. Matt. 11:25; Luke 10:21] to sin, it would be better for him to have a great millstone fastened around his neck and to be drowned in the depth of the sea. . . . See that you do not despise *one of these little ones.* For I tell you that in heaven their angels always see the face of my Father who is in heaven. What do you think? If a man has a hundred sheep, and one of them has gone astray, does he not leave the ninety-nine on the mountains and go in search of the one that went astray?

And if he finds it, truly, I say to you, he rejoices over it more than over the ninety-nine that never went astray. So it is not the will of my Father who is in heaven that *one of these little ones* should perish." (Matt. 18:2–14; see also Matt. 11:25–26; Luke 10:21)

Though there is a common tie that binds all the children of Adam, the mutual link between the children of God is more holy.

—John Calvin

When the Son of Man comes in his glory, and all the angels with him, then he will sit on his glorious throne. Before him will be gathered all the nations, and he will separate people one from another as a shepherd separates the sheep from the goats. And he will place the sheep on his right, but the goats on the left. Then the King will say to those on his right, "Come, you who are blessed by my Father, inherit the kingdom prepared for you from the foundation of the world. For I was hungry and you gave me food, I was thirsty and you gave me drink, I was a stranger and you welcomed me, I was naked and you clothed me, I was sick and you visited me, I was in prison and you came to me." Then the righteous will answer him, saying, "Lord, when did we see you hungry and feed you, or thirsty and give you drink? And when did we see you a stranger and welcome you, or naked and clothe you? And when did we see you sick or in prison and visit you?" And the King will answer them, "Truly, I say to you, as you did it to *one of the least of these my brothers, you did it to me*." Then he will say to those on his left, "Depart from me, you cursed, into the eternal fire prepared for the devil and his angels. For I was hungry and you gave me no food, I was thirsty and you gave me no drink, I was a stranger and you did not welcome me, naked and you did not clothe me, sick and in prison and you did not visit me." Then they also will answer, saying, "Lord, when did we see you hungry or thirsty or a stranger or naked or sick or in prison, and did not minister to you?" Then he will answer them, saying, "Truly, I say to you, as you did not do it to *one of the least of these, you did not do it to me.*" And these will go away into eternal punishment, but the righteous into eternal life. (Matt. 25:31–46)

Truly, truly, I say to you, whoever *receives the one I send receives me*, and whoever receives me receives the one who sent me. (John 13:20)

But take care that this right of yours does not somehow become a stumbling block to the weak. For if anyone sees you who have knowledge eating in an idol's temple, will he not be encouraged, if his conscience is weak, to eat food offered to idols? And so by your knowledge this weak person is destroyed, the brother for whom Christ died. Thus, *sinning against your brothers and wounding their conscience when it is weak, you sin against Christ.* (1 Cor. 8:9–12)

The Appropriate Context. This is the biblical and theological context within which Matthew 25:31–46 belongs. When Jesus speaks there of "the least of these my brothers," he is not referring to just any poor person. There is no biblical warrant for supposing that people become Jesus's brothers or one of his "little ones" simply by becoming hungry, or thirsty, or impoverished, or incarcerated in prison (see also Matt. 12:49–50; 28:10; Heb. 2:10–18). Nor does the Bible teach that such individuals somehow embody Jesus in the world. Jesus surely is embodied in the world, but according to the New Testament, including Matthew 25, he is embodied in his followers (Col. 2:19), his brothers, his disciples, his little ones who believe, even "the least of them." To broaden this notion of embodiment to include anyone who may be suffering is to take a dramatic step beyond the clear biblical witness, one which does a disservice not only to Matthew 25 but to every one of the above passages.

Must we say it again? None of this is designed to call into question God's unique compassion for those who are suffering. It may be something of an overstatement to speak of his so-called preference for the poor,[4] since no such universal category as "the poor" is discernable in the Scriptures; the biblical testimony about poverty is too nuanced for that. But we should not question that God is profoundly affected by human need. Jesus came into the world in the lowliest of stations and lived his entire life among the poor. He wept for his suffering friends and enemies alike and gave himself on the cross to heal a hurting, broken humanity. None can question God's deep compassion for and identification with those who are destitute and vulnerable, wherever they may be found.

But this is not the message of Matthew 25. To make it the message of Matthew 25 is to distract us from the more focused point Jesus wanted his listeners to understand. This passage should be viewed as a counterpart to what the apostle Paul discovered on the road to Damascus. Jesus is informing us that whatever we do to his people, for good or ill, we do to him. If anything, Matthew 25 is a call to serve Christ today by laying ourselves on the line for our fellow believers, more of whom may be suffering for their association with Jesus in our generation than at any time in history.[5] Blunting Jesus's point by broadening it out to include all human suffering, however well-intentioned, does not merely miss Jesus's point; it undermines and falsifies it. It's a classic violation of what N. T. Wright has called "the double rule of good exegesis":

> First, we must pay attention to the text against all our traditions, however venerable their provenance and however pastorally helpful we find them. Second, if we do not do this, but rather (even unwittingly) allow our traditions to force us to read the text in a way which it does not in fact support, that means that there is something the text really does want to tell us which we are muzzling, denying, not allowing to come out.[6]

CONCLUSION

Our quest for a biblical balance between "word and deed" must begin with a commitment to treat the Bible with integrity. Even the best of motives will not justify forcing biblical texts to say something they were never intended to say. We must discipline ourselves to handle the Scriptures carefully, trusting them to "train us in righteousness." Only then will we become the people Jesus calls us to be, a people thoroughly "equipped for every good work" (2 Tim. 3:16–17).

CONCLUSION

PUTTING IT TOGETHER

A hungry belly has no ears.

—Japanese proverb

According to the Bible, God's people are called to both verbal and nonverbal witness in the world. What do the Scriptures tell us about these two forms of witness? How do they relate to each other and how can we remain faithful to both? These are the questions we have explored throughout this book.

I have argued that the stakes in this discussion are high. This is not some abstract debate only distantly related to how we live. The issue is our faithful obedience to Jesus Christ, an obedience which must begin with clear thinking about what he's calling us to be and do. As I noted in the introduction, if we do not understand our calling, or if we are operating with a distorted vision of that calling, faithful obedience is not likely to be the outcome. This is why generating clear, biblical answers to the above questions is of genuine importance.

Yet we must also acknowledge that even the clearest grasp of our biblical calling does not guarantee simple, straightforward (much less *easy*) answers in real-life situations. Our biblical categories and priorities may be crystal clear in the abstract, but how do we apply them in our complicated dealings with flesh-and-blood people?[1] Every man and woman, not to mention every collection of men and women, represents a complex jumble of human needs, needs the church's words and deeds are called to serve. How do we decide in any given situation what is needed most?

One of the questions we sometimes run across in the "word versus deed" discussion—whether it is raised openly or remains below the surface—is which of these is most important. Should we emphasize a verbal witness in our ministry or our nonverbal witness? The appropriate answer must surely be, it depends. Final answers to such a question will not be found in the abstract. To answer it we must abandon the conceptual realm and submit ourselves to the people before us. In the end, the question of which is most important, word or deed, can only be answered in concrete human situations, in light of the full range of needs we discover there.

A BIBLICAL VIEW OF HUMAN NEED

For a Christian, any useful analysis of human needs must begin with a biblical understanding of the human person. What are human beings? Are they, despite illusions to the contrary, nothing more than physical creatures, as materialists would have us believe? Or are they complex, comprised of body and spirit? Or perhaps body, soul, and spirit? Such questions have long been debated, with most Christian thinkers landing on some variation of the latter options. But however we answer the question, if we are thinking biblically we will wind up, in one way or the other, conceiving of human beings as complex *unities* where heaven and earth meet.

Following Plato, many ancient Greek, not to mention later Gnostic and Manichean, thinkers viewed reality as dualistic. The visible material world is evil or dark, while the invisible spiritual world is good and filled with light. The human self or soul is related to the spiritual world. Unfortunately it is also trapped in the prison of a physical body. Salvation therefore consists of the soul's escape from its material bondage back to the ethereal realm of the spiritual, its true home. A biblical view of humans, by contrast, is rather different.

According to the Bible a human being is a *nephesh* (Heb., "soul") consisting of creaturely flesh animated by the breath of God himself (Gen. 2:7). The term *nephesh* refers not to some immaterial part of us but to what we are: living creatures of God. We were designed by God as part of his creation—a creation he repeatedly pronounced "good" and which he is in the process of redeeming—and we remain part

> You don't have a soul. You are a Soul. You have a body.
> —C. S. Lewis

of it. Our destiny is not to escape that creation in order to know God, but the reverse: God came to us. He took upon himself flesh, dignifying the created order in the person of Jesus Christ so as to redeem both us and the world he made. Our future is not that of disembodied souls who have escaped to some purely spiritual realm. We will spend eternity as resurrected, re-embodied persons inhabiting God's redeemed, glorified creation, enjoying both it and him forever. Our resurrection bodies will be changed from their present state, to be sure, but they will be glorified versions of the bodies we now inhabit, as was our Lord's.

This biblical view of the human person requires us to call into question any notion that says God cares only about whisking disembodied souls out of this sinful world into some otherworldly existence called "heaven." God made us for fellowship with himself, but it was precisely as earthly creatures that he did so. Sin—our mutiny against God's sovereign rule—became a barrier to that fellowship. But our earthliness itself was never the problem. To suppose otherwise is to embrace an ancient Greek anthropology, not the Bible's—and to court christological heresy. God designed humans as complex yet unified earthly creatures capable of union and spiritual fellowship with him. Keeping this in mind can help us make better sense of our "word versus deed" calling in the world.

PRIORITIZING WORD AND DEED

We have been at pains throughout this book to shape our thinking about "word and deed" according to the Bible's categories, out of a conviction that conceptual clarity here is important if we are to be faithful to Christ's calling.

But now let's reverse the poles. With our biblical priorities in place, let us approach the question from the ground up. How do we prioritize our "word versus deed" responsibilities in the wear and tear of life? Which is the more important, not theoretically now but in practice? The following is a three-step approach that does justice both to our biblical priorities and the unique needs of the human beings with which we deal.

Think for a moment not of people in general but of one specific person, someone to whom you might conceivably have an opportunity to minister in Christ's name. Perhaps you will imagine a friend, a relative, your doctor or teacher, an AIDS sufferer in Sub-Saharan Africa, an inner-city child, a peasant in Central America, a prominent politician, a girl held as a sex slave in East Asia, your pastor, or a soldier in a war zone. It may be anyone, but choose just one specific person. Then ask the following (successively more concrete) questions about that person:

1) What are this person's needs?
This question can be answered fairly easily in the abstract. We are all God's creatures, and he has made us with identifiable needs. It would not be difficult to demonstrate that, according to the Scriptures, the person you have in mind has at least these types of needs:

- physical
- emotional
- intellectual
- social
- spiritual

Thus our first question is fairly easily addressed. Whoever you have imagined, you may count on the fact that, given how God has made us, that person experiences needs in each of these areas. No one can escape them. They are a part of the human condition. This leads to the second question.

> Humans are amphibians—half spirit and half animal. As spirits they belong to the eternal world, but as animals they inhabit time.
> —C. S. Lewis

2) What are your person's "most important" needs?

This query, now, is less easily answered. How might we reorder the above list according to importance? Volumes could be—have been!—written about such things, and we will not resolve the issues in these pages. But since in this question we are still dealing at a fairly abstract level, on the basis of the testimony of Scripture two things can certainly be said.

First, however we might reorder this list, your person's spiritual needs will always ratchet to the top. Are a man's social needs greater than his intellectual needs? Are a woman's physical needs more important than her emotional needs? Such questions would rightly engender not only a lively debate but also, quite likely, a healthy resistance to any such forced ranking. But on the testimony of Jesus himself we can affirm this: if we are ordering these needs according to their "importance," the person's spiritual needs will always rank first. This is not because, as noted earlier, the spiritual is more important than the material, but because what is eternal is more important than the temporal.

The Bible is clear that a person's greatest need is to come into right relationship with God through Jesus Christ, his Son. Apart from Christ, "it is a fearful thing to fall into the hands of the living God" (Heb. 10:31). As has sometimes been observed, salvation in the Bible is salvation *by* God and *for* God—but also *from God*. As Jesus himself put it:

> I tell you, my friends, do not fear those who kill the body, and after that have nothing more that they can do. But I will warn you whom to fear: fear him who, after he has killed, has authority to cast into hell. Yes, I tell you, fear him! (Luke 12:4–5; see also Matt. 10:28)

What need could surpass this one? According to Jesus, even the need for physical safety pales when compared to a person's spiritual need to know God and escape his divine judgment; the need to pass from eternal death to eternal life (John 3:16–18); the need to be "justified by faith" in order to discover "peace with God through our Lord Jesus Christ" and the "hope of the glory of God" (Rom. 5:1–2); the need to be "delivered . . . from the domain of darkness and transferred . . . to the kingdom of his beloved Son, in whom we have redemption, the forgiveness of sins" (Col. 1:13–14; see also Acts 10:43). John Newton said it beautifully: "T'was grace that taught my heart to fear / and grace my fears relieved. / How precious did that grace appear / the hour I first believed!" However else our list may look once we have reordered it, a person's spiritual need must inevitably rise to the top.

Yet the second thing we can know for certain, also on the basis of Scripture, is that this spiritual need does not exist in isolation. Your person is a *unified* creation of God. He or she will have any number of other needs, each of which is designed by God and none of which are hermetically sealed from the others. Each of these other needs potentially interacts with your person's spiritual needs while also impinging on one another. God has built this person as a complex, *unified* creature with many legitimate needs. What's more, he cares about each need. He loves the *whole person*, not just his or her "soul." And he calls us to do the same. This is what makes our third question so important.

3) What are your person's "most urgent" needs?
Now we are no longer dealing in the abstract; we are trying to understand how we can best serve this person in the light of his or her actual life situation. This requires us to rethink our list once more.

Imagine again the person you have in mind. God calls you to serve his or her needs, the greatest of which is to know him through Christ. But you also see that his or her other needs are real and legitimate, and like Jesus himself, you want to care for the *whole person*. So what does this require of you? It's a question that cannot be answered in the abstract. We can only raise this question amidst the specific circumstances of your individual's life. How we think through its answer will depend on at least two determining factors.

Most obviously, it will depend on *your grasp of this person's unique needs*. We are called to both word and deed in Christ's service. So which does this person need from you? Which is the more urgent? Which can you address? Which is not in your power to address? Consider, for instance, how your answer might vary depending on whom you have in mind:

- An African villager dying of hunger, or thirst, or AIDS may desperately need a verbal witness of the good news of Jesus; but he may also need food, water, or a cocktail of anti-viral drugs before he will be in any condition even to hear the gospel.

- A woman down the street who is going through a divorce may be angry at God, but she still needs a friend to share her pain until she can heal enough to receive Christ's love.

- A stranger beside you on a plane may be primed by the Holy Spirit for a clear verbal witness of the gospel, followed by the establishment of a caring long-distance discipling relationship.

- A group of people who are suffering injustice may need us to stand up for them whether or not we ever have the opportunity to share the gospel with them.

- A lonely teenager with few friends may need a patient, enduring friendship that models the love and grace of Jesus, leading ultimately, as God gives the opportunity, to a verbal witness of the gospel.

- A Christian friend who has lost a beloved child may need most not our words but our presence, along with practical help in just getting through the day.

- A panhandler on the street may need an investment not only of our money but of our time and interest as we take him into a restaurant for a meal and a caring conversation.

- An unbelieving but inquiring neighbor attending an evangelistic Bible study in our home may need a clear explanation of how he can come to know God through Christ.

- A complacent loved one who has everything and has repeatedly heard the gospel from us may need to be loved in silence for a while.

So which is more important, our words or our deeds? As these examples demonstrate, the question cannot be answered in the abstract. Our answer must vary in practice from person to person, situation to situation, from one time to another.

Second, and perhaps less obviously, our answer must also depend on *our particular calling from the Lord.*

It is sometimes said that the church is not called to solve all of society's ills, and this must certainly be true. One day God himself will wipe away every tear. There will be no more death or grief or pain or suffering (Rev. 21:4). Only then will all of society's ills be healed. In the meantime, however, the world will know far more human need than we can meet. Jesus calls his church to a ministry of word and deed in serving that need, but this cannot mean that he has called any of us, or even all of us, to satisfy *all* of that need. Merely putting the thought into words demonstrates its absurdity. No mere mortal or group of mortals could fulfill such a calling. We must take recourse instead to what we may call the "Nehemiah Principle."

> It may at first sound counterintuitive, but in the end it is powerfully liberating to realize that God does not expect us to respond every time we see a need. A need is not a call.

The Nehemiah Principle. Nehemiah faced a daunting task, one that appeared beyond his reach. His rebuilding the city of Jerusalem required him to erect a massive defensive wall within a short period of time. It seemed impossible. Yet to everyone's surprise the wall went up. Nehemiah assigned different families, clans, and individuals their own sections of the wall. When each party fulfilled its particular assignment, the wall became a reality (Neh. 6:15).

The Nehemiah Principle suggests that while none of us can do *everything*, all of us can do and are called to do *something*. So what is the *something* God is calling us to do? Our question must always be, what part of the task is Christ calling me to fulfill?

It may at first sound counterintuitive, but in the end it is powerfully liberating to realize that God does not expect us to respond every time we see a need. We can render this point in a simple axiom: *A need is not a call.* The needs of the world, whether for our words or our deeds, will far outstrip our ability to meet them. It is therefore impossible for us to meet every need; only God can bear such a burden. Attempting to respond to every worthy need, and then experiencing guilt and despair when we inevitably prove inadequate, is a prescription for failure and burnout. We are trying to do what only God can do.

> Your neighbor may not care how much you know, until he knows how much you care.
> —Anonymous

Far better is to make our decisions not on the basis of human needs, however legitimate they may be, but on the basis of God's *call*. We cannot do everything, but we can do *something*. Of the seemingly limitless needs in the world, which is God calling me to address? In other words, what is my part of the wall? Answering this question can prevent us from throwing up our hands in frustration and defeat when the world's needs vastly outstrip our ability to meet them. We must let God be God and then focus on the sacrificial tasks to which he has called us.

Costly Service. The term *sacrificial* is an important one. Coming to understand and accept our limitations does not relieve us from costly service. As we spend ourselves and our resources in building our part of the wall we must be willing to do so sacrificially for Christ's sake and for the sake of those to whom he calls us. Learning to respond to call rather than need is not a technique for escaping costly service; it's a plan for avoiding false guilt.

Genuine feelings of guilt can be healthy. They are our conscience at work. They are what we experience when we've done what we ought not to have done or not done what we should have done (Rom. 14:22). But *false* guilt is worse than worthless; it's toxic. False guilt is what we experience when we try to operate unreflectively on the unspoken premise that every need is automatically a call. This is a presumptions idea, one which assumes we possess Godlike capacities rather than creaturely limitations. Treating every need as a call is a sure-fire prescription for the discouragement and frustration that arise when we inevitably fall short in our efforts to accomplish what God never expected, enabled, or called us to do.

In our generation of instant worldwide communication, we are daily witnesses to far more human need than any previous generation could have imagined. Yet we can never do everything even in one situation of need, much less in all of them. We will quickly be overwhelmed if we try to respond to every need we see. Inevitably we must leave the larger task in the all-powerful hands of God, determined all the while to be faithful in building the section of the wall he has assigned us. This is how it must be for all who are truly God's fellow workers:

> I planted, Apollos watered, but God gave the growth. So neither he who plants nor he who waters is anything, but only God who gives the growth. He who plants and he who waters are one, and each will receive his wages according to his labor. For we are God's fellow workers. (1 Cor. 3:6–9)

Following the wooing of Christ's call rather than allowing ourselves to be driven by false guilt is a far more satisfying, and more biblical, way of living the Christian life. It's the only spiritually, emotionally, and physically healthy way to function as God's fellow workers in Christ's kingdom.

Now may our Lord Jesus Christ himself, and God our Father, who loved us and gave us eternal comfort and good hope through grace, comfort your hearts and establish them in every good work and word.

—2 Thessalonians 2:16–17

NOTES

Introduction

1. In speaking of the Christian's calling or mission, I will sometimes use the term *church* as loosely interchangeable with *Christians*, *God's people*, or the *body of Christ*. Were we to speak more technically, we might wish to maintain a distinction between the church's mandate and that of individual Christians. See, e.g., Michael Horton, *The Gospel Commission: Recovering God's Strategy for Making Disciples* (Grand Rapids, MI: Baker, 2011), 210–46.

2. We should not press this point unduly, however. As one Franciscan source observes, even if this saying did not come from Francis himself it's "a great quote, [and is] very Franciscan in its spirit. . . . In Chapter XVII of his Rule of 1221, Francis told the friars not to preach unless they had received the proper permission to do so. Then he added, 'Let all the brothers, however, preach by their deeds.'"

Chapter 2: The Gospel Is Verbal

1. See his *Apostleship*, trans. and ed. J. R. Coates (London: Adam & Charles Black, 1952).

2. "ἀπòστολος," *Theological Dictionary of the New Testament*, ed. G. Kittel, trans. G. W. Bromiley (Grand Rapids, MI: Eerdmans, 1965), 1:431.

3. Rengstorf, *Apostleship*, 436.

4. Not for the first time. See Mark 1:4; Luke 16:16; Acts 13:24–25; Gal. 3:8.

5. Speaking verbs are used a few times metaphorically in the Old Testament, e.g., "The heavens *declare* the glory of God, and the sky above *proclaims* his handiwork" (Ps. 19:1). The respective speaking verbs here are *caphar* and *nagad* in the Hebrew and *diegeomai* and *apaggello* in the Greek translation (LXX). Yet notice what is being "declared" via this non-verbal channel. It is the very sort of thing we have said nonverbal channels are especially effective at communicating: that a creator exists and he is astonishingly powerful. According to the apostle Paul, "[God's] invisible attributes, namely, his eternal power and divine nature, have been clearly perceived, ever since the creation of the world, in the things that have been made" (Rom. 1:20). Such a message can indeed be communicated

via deeds, in the same way our deeds "declare" to others that we exist and provide insight into what we are like. See also the metaphor of writing in 2 Cor. 3:2–3.

6. First Cor. 11:26 might seem an exception: "For as often as you eat this bread and drink the cup, you proclaim [*kataggelo*] the Lord's death until he comes." But the symbolic act of partaking in the Lord's Supper does not qualify as truly "nonverbal" behavior. Eating and drinking, in and of themselves, obviously do not communicate the gospel; apart from a verbalized account of some sort, the mere eating of bread and drinking of wine conveys no such message. The bread and wine of the Lord's Table are unique symbols, the profound meaning of which requires verbal expression. Once that explanation is in place, the symbols can announce or point to that verbal meaning. But this symbolic function renders the elements more akin to sign language than to true nonverbal behavior, which is nonsymbolic.

Chapter 3: Evangelism Is Verbal

1. "The Two Tasks," address, Wheaton College, Wheaton, IL (1980); see also "The Two Tasks," *Journal of the Evangelical Theological Society*, vol. 24 (December 1980): 289–96; *The Two Tasks of the Christian Scholar: Redeeming the Soul, Redeeming the Mind*, ed. William Lane Craig and Paul M. Gould (Wheaton, IL: Crossway, 2007).

2. For a fuller treatment of this subject, see Duane Litfin, *St. Paul's Theology of Proclamation: 1 Corinthians 1–4 and Greco-Roman Rhetoric*, vol. 79, SNTS Monograph Series (Cambridge: Cambridge University Press, 1994); or Duane Litfin, "Swallowing Our Pride: An Essay on the Foolishness of Preaching," in *Preach the Word: Essays on Expository Preaching in Honor of R. Kent Hughes*, ed. Leland Ryken and Todd Wilson (Wheaton, IL: Crossway, 2007).

3. C. K. Barrett, *A Commentary on the First Epistle to the Corinthians*, Harper's New Testament Commentaries (New York: Harper & Row, 1968), 51.

Chapter 4: Abstractions and Their Uses

1. See Wendell Johnson, *People in Quandaries: The Semantics of Personal Adjustment* (New York: Harper & Brothers, 1946), 151.

2. C. S. Lewis, "Transposition," in *The Weight of Glory*, ed. Walter Hooper (New York: Collier, 1980), 71.

3. Johnson, *People in Quandaries*, 270.

4. Samuel Ichiye Hayakawa, *Language and Thought in Action* (New York: Harcourt Brace Jovanovich, 1978), 164.

5. Johnson, *People in Quandaries*, 273.

6. Hayakawa, *Language and Thought in Action*, 166.

7. In technical philosophical terms, abstractions are high order super-collective nouns. Rather than limiting ourselves to this technical

definition, however, in what follows I will use the ladder of abstraction more loosely to refer not only to abstractions proper but also to such things as general ideas and their particular implications, or large theological affirmations and their specific applications or entailments.

8. Richard M. Weaver, *Ideas Have Consequences* (Chicago: University of Chicago Press, 1984).

Chapter 5: Theology Applied

1. An *entailment* is a required or necessary accompaniment or consequence.

2. It is significant that Jesus regularly paired this affirmation with the parallel requirement to love our neighbors as ourselves: "[A] lawyer stood up to put him to the test, saying, 'Teacher, what shall I do to inherit eternal life?' [Jesus] said to him, 'What is written in the Law? How do you read it?' And [the lawyer] answered, 'You shall love the Lord your God with all your heart and with all your soul and with all your strength and with all your mind, and your neighbor as yourself.' And [Jesus] said to him, 'You have answered correctly; do this, and you will live'" (Luke 10:25–28; see also 2 Kings 23:25; Matt. 22:37–40; Mark 12:29–31). As has often been observed, neither Jesus nor James espoused a doctrine of faith *plus* works but rather a view of genuine faith as something more than mere mental assent: a faith *that* works. In other words, saving faith is inevitably of the sort, if it is genuine, that expresses itself externally in gospel-worthy behavior.

Chapter 6: Gospel-Worthy Deeds

1. Due to the profound example of Christ's own coming into the world (e.g., Phil. 2:6–8), the notion of incarnation is a crucial one for Christians. On the other hand, I will avoid the confusing term *incarnational evangelism*. By conflating *incarnation* with *evangelism* the resulting term encourages the misguided notion that we can "preach the gospel" by our lives; that is, that by faithfully living out the gospel's implications we are thereby proclaiming the gospel itself. As we have seen, this cannot be the case. The gospel is inherently a verbal thing, and evangelism is inherently a verbal behavior.

2. Though, as Bruce Waltke observes, "The biblical authors did not favor endogamous marriages ["marriage within a particular group in accordance with custom or law"] over exogamous ones provided that the foreign wife left her pagan society and embraced the faith of true Israel (cf. Ps 45:10–15)." *The Book of Proverbs, Chapters 1–15*, New International Commentary on the Old Testament (Grand Rapids, MI: Eerdmans, 2004), 122.

3. "As presented in the Bible itself, [the Old Testament laws] were understood to have been intended for the instruction or direction of the people of Israel, not as laws for other peoples either during the biblical

period or in later times." Richard H. Hiers, *Justice and Compassion in Biblical Law* (New York: Continuum, 2009), 2.

4. See Mark 9:41–42; Acts 11:29–30; 24:17; Rom. 15:25–26; 1 Cor. 12:12–27; Gal. 2:8–10; 2 Tim. 1:15–17; Heb. 13:3; 6:10.

5. "The Cape Town Commitment," The Lausanne Movement (2011), 10, A, http://www.lausanne.org/en/documents/ctcommitment.html#p1-8.

6. Ibid.

Chapter 7: Living Wisely

1. Bruce Waltke, *The Book of Proverbs, Chapters 1–15*, New International Commentary on the Old Testament (Grand Rapids, MI: Eerdmans, 2004), 126.

Chapter 8: Obeying the King

1. Timothy Keller, *Generous Justice: How God's Grace Makes Us Just* (New York: Dutton, 2010), 67.

2. For an exploration of this indirect approach to communication, modeled after Jesus, see Raymond Anderson, "Kierkegaard's Theory of Communication," Speech Monographs 30 (1963): 1–14.

3. "And when his disciples asked him what this parable meant, he said, 'To you it has been given to know the secrets of the kingdom of God, but for others they are in parables, so that "seeing they may not see, and hearing they may not understand"'" (Luke 8:9–10; see also Matt. 13:10–17; Mark 4:10–12). Jesus's inclination to communicate via indirection was a form of judgment on unbelief, one that frustrated his opponents (John 10:24). Even his disciples were relieved when he abandoned this mode and began speaking to them "plainly" (John 16:25–30).

4. *The Weight of Glory and Other Addresses*, ed. Walter Hooper (New York: Macmillan, 1949), 18–19.

Chapter 9: Serving the Kingdom

1. This emphasis was expressed in the classic language of the Lausanne Covenant (1974) as follows: "We affirm that there is only one Saviour and only one gospel. . . . We recognise that everyone has some knowledge of God through his general revelation in nature. But we deny that this can save, for people suppress the truth by their unrighteousness. We also reject as derogatory to Christ and the gospel every kind of syncretism and dialogue which implies that Christ speaks equally through all religions and ideologies. Jesus Christ, being himself the only God-man, who gave himself as the only ransom for sinners, is the only mediator between God and people. There is no other name by which we must be saved. All men and women are perishing because of sin, but God loves everyone, not wishing that any should perish but that all should repent. Yet those who reject Christ repudiate the joy of salvation and condemn

themselves to eternal separation from God. To proclaim Jesus as "the Saviour of the world" is not to affirm that all people are either automatically or ultimately saved, still less to affirm that all religions offer salvation in Christ. Rather it is to proclaim God's love for a world of sinners and to invite everyone to respond to him as Saviour and Lord in the whole-hearted personal commitment of repentance and faith."

2. Christopher J. H. Wright, *The Mission of God's People: A Biblical Theology of the Church's Mission* (Grand Rapids, MI: Zondervan, 2010), 41.

3. This emphasis too was well-expressed in the 1974 Lausanne Covenant: "We affirm that God is both the Creator and the Judge of all people. We therefore should share his concern for justice and reconciliation throughout human society and for the liberation of men and women from every kind of oppression. Because men and women are made in the image of God, every person, regardless of race, religion, colour, culture, class, sex or age, has an intrinsic dignity because of which he or she should be respected and served, not exploited. Here too we express penitence both for our neglect and for having sometimes regarded evangelism and social concern as mutually exclusive. Although reconciliation with other people is not reconciliation with God, nor is social action evangelism, nor is political liberation salvation, nevertheless we affirm that evangelism and socio-political involvement are both part of our Christian duty. For both are necessary expressions of our doctrines of God and man, our love for our neighbour and our obedience to Jesus Christ. The message of salvation implies also a message of judgment upon every form of alienation, oppression and discrimination, and we should not be afraid to denounce evil and injustice wherever they exist. When people receive Christ they are born again into his kingdom and must seek not only to exhibit but also to spread its righteousness in the midst of an unrighteous world. The salvation we claim should be transforming us in the totality of our personal and social responsibilities. Faith without works is dead."

4. John Stott, *Christian Mission in the Modern World* (Downers Grove, IL: InterVarsity, 2008), 48.

5. James Davison Hunter, *To Change the World: The Irony, Tragedy, and Possibility of Christianity in the Late Modern World* (Oxford: Oxford University Press, 2010), 233.

6. Though, we should note, the Greek term *soteria* ("salvation") in the New Testament focuses almost exclusively on the notion of "salvation from." See Werner Foerster, "σῴζω, σωτηρία," *Theological Dictionary of the New Testament*, ed. Gerhard Friedrich and Geoffrey W. Bromiley (Grand Rapids, MI: Eerdmans, 1971), 7:1002–3.

7. "God in the Dock," in *God in the Dock: Essays on Theology and Ethics*, ed. Walter Hooper (Grand Rapids, MI: Eerdmans, 1970), 244. "God in the Dock" was the editor's title for this essay, but Lewis's original

title was more revealing: "Difficulties in Presenting the Christian Faith to Modern Unbelievers."

8. Francis Thompson's famous poem *Hound of Heaven,* http://www.houndsofheaven.com/thepoem.htm.

9. "And Can It Be That I Should Gain?" (1738).

10. Walter Brueggemann, *Peace* (St. Louis, MO: Chalice Press, 2001), 13.

Chapter 10: Adorning the Gospel

1. Aristotle, *Rhetoric,* 1.2.3–7.

2. Aristides, *Apology,* 15.

3. Tertullian, *Apology,* 39.57–59.

4. Matthew Parris, "As an Atheist, I Truly Believe Africa Needs God," *Times* (London), December 27, 2008.

Chapter 11: Stewarding the Creation

1. Douglas J. Moo, "Eschatology and Environmental Ethics: On the Importance of Biblical Theology to Creation Care," in *Keeping God's Earth: The Global Environment in Biblical Perspective,* ed. Noah J. Toly and Daniel L. Block (Downers Grove, IL: InterVarsity, 2010), 35.

2. E.g., Toly and Block, *Keeping God's Earth*; Lindy Stott, ed., *Christians, the Care of Creation and Global Climate Change* (Eugene, OR: Pickwick, 2008); Steven Bouma-Predige, *For the Beauty of the Earth: A Christian Vision for Creation Care,* 2nd ed. (Grand Rapids, MI: Baker Academic, 2010); Jonathan Merritt, *Green Like God: Unlocking the Divine Plan for Our Planet* (Nashville, TN: Faith Words, 2010); Scott C. Sabin, *Tending to Eden: Environmental Stewardship for God's People* (Valley Forge, PA: Judson Press, 2010); Matthew Sleeth, *The Gospel according to the Earth: Why the Good Book Is a Green Book* (New York: HarperOne, 2010).

Chapter 12: Rightly Dividing the Word

1. This distinction was the rule, but justice also required appropriate exceptions, e.g., "You shall not oppress a hired worker who is poor and needy, whether he is one of your brothers or one of the sojourners who are in your land within your towns. You shall give him his wages on the same day, before the sun sets (for he is poor and counts on it), lest he cry against you to the LORD, and you be guilty of sin" (Deut. 24:14–15; see also vv. 17–22; on the negative side, see Lev. 24:22). Sojourners (foreigners who worshiped with Israel) were another exception; they bore the same sacrificial requirements as Israelites (Num. 15:14–16).

2. See Isa. 3:14–15; 10:2; 58:1; Jer. 5:26–28; 22:13–17; Ezek. 16:1, 49; 22:29; Amos 2:7; 4:1; 5:11–12; 8:4–6; Zech. 7:8–14. "Your own flesh" in Isa. 58:7 is sometimes mistakenly read as a reference to humanity in general. But in the Old Testament, the term "your flesh" (*basar*), when not used of the physical body ("The Philistine said to David, 'Come to

me, and I will give your flesh to the birds of the air and to the beasts of the field'" [1 Sam. 17:44]), denotes Jewish brotherhood: "Then all Israel gathered together to David at Hebron and said, 'Behold, we are your bone and flesh'" (1 Chron. 11:1; see also Judg. 9:1–2; 2 Sam. 5:1). "All flesh" is the term used when the reference is to humanity in general (Gen. 6:12; Num. 18:15; Job 34:15; see also Isa. 66:16, 24).

3. For instance, while all will agree that Christians should work toward *justice*, not all are agreed on what that means. The issues are not as straight-forward as they may seem. See, e.g., Alasdair MacIntyre, *Whose Justice? Which Rationality?* (Notre Dame, IN: University of Notre Dame Press, 1988); or Michael Sandel, *Justice: What's the Right Thing to Do?* (New York: Farrar, Straus & Giroux, 2009); or Nicholas Wolterstorff, *Justice: Rights and Wrongs* (Princeton, NJ: Princeton University Press, 2008).

4. This was George Eldon Ladd's point when he famously said, "There is little explicit teaching on social ethics in the Gospels." *The Presence of the Future: The Eschatology of Biblical Realism* (Grand Rapids, MI: Eerdmans, 1974), 303.

Chapter 13: Three Key Passages

1. The marriages envisioned here were apparently marriages within the exile community, not intermarriages with the Babylonians. In this regard, as in every other, the Israelites were to remain faithful to God's law (Deut. 7:1–5; Ezra 9–10; cf. Gen. 24:3). Like the four young men in Daniel 1, the exiles were to make the best of their difficult situation with-out compromising their allegiance to Israel's God or disobeying his word. A failure to do so was what prompted their exile in the first place.

2. *Mere Christianity*, bk. 2, chap. 3, para. 7.

3. "The Babylonians, all the Chaldeans. . . . I will delegate judgment to them, and they shall judge you according to their judgments" (Ezek. 23:23–24, NKJV). God similarly used Nebuchadnezzar to judge Egypt (Ezek. 29:19; 30:10–11, 24–25).

4. This phrase grew out of the Liberation Theology movements of the 1960s. It was designed to highlight God's special care for those who are suffering under social, economic, and political oppression. "Preference for the poor means that even though God loves all people, he identifies with the poor, reveals himself to the poor and sides with the poor in a spe-cial way. Above all, it means that in the class struggle God sides with the poor against every oppressor who would exploit or dehumanize them." Stanley J. Grenz and Roger E. Olson, *20th Century Theology: God and the World in a Transitional Age* (Downers Grove, IL: InterVarsity, 1992), 218. To speak of God's "preference for the poor" is well-intended but also misleading. As we have seen, not all the poor are objects of God's prefer-ence. Poverty may be the result of foolishness or rebellion, while wealth may be the product of godly wisdom (Prov. 8:12, 18). God sometimes

blesses the one who has and disciplines the one who has not: "If any-one is not willing to work, let him not eat" (2 Thess. 3:10). But more importantly, the issues at stake strike deeper than this phrase suggests. The Bible's universal warning about wealth is not that it is evil but that it is seductive and spiritually corrosive. The temptation, as always, is to human pride. Wealth, and the power that typically travels with it, often deceive and corrupt (Matt. 13:22; Mark 4:9; 1 Tim. 6:9–10), making it harder for the rich and powerful to humble themselves in dependence on God (Mark 10:22–25). The poor, by contrast, are far more conscious of their need and thus more willing to entrust themselves to God. According to the Bible, God refuses to accommodate human pride. He "prefers," therefore, to bypass the proud and achieve his purposes through those who lack status and power in the world. The issue is not that the poor are the neediest and thus first in line for God's care; an infinite God scarcely needs us to queue for his attention. There is something larger and more significant at stake. God chooses "what is foolish in the world to shame the wise; . . . what is weak in the world to shame the strong; . . . what is low and despised in the world, even things that are not, to bring to noth-ing things that are, so that no human being might boast in the presence of God" (1 Cor. 1:27–29, see also Matt. 11:25–26). "Listen, my beloved brothers," says James, "has not God chosen those who are poor in the world to be rich in faith and heirs of the kingdom, which he has promised to those who love him?" (2:5). If we may speak at all of a divine "prefer-ence for the poor," it's not simply that the poor are materially lacking; God is drawn to the poor because it is from their number that he typically finds those willing to abandon themselves to him in love and faith, without which it is "impossible to please him" (Heb. 11:6). This was the underly-ing issue in Jesus's repeated admonition: "Many who are first will be last, and the last first" (see Matt. 19:30; 29:16; Mark 9:35; 10:31; Luke 13:30).

5. See http://www.persecution.org/; http://www.opendoorsusa.org/. The following organizations are also serving the persecuted church: Christian Freedom International, Christian Solidarity Worldwide, Christians in Crisis, Compassion Radio, Fishhook International, Gospel for Asia, Greater Calling, International Christian Concern, Iranian Christians International, Jubilee Campaign, Mission India, Project Foundation, The Voice of the Martyrs, World Bible Translation Center, World Evangelical Alliance, The Last Harvest.

6. N. T. Wright, *Justification: God's Plan and Paul's Vision* (Downers Grove, IL: InterVarsity, 2009), 159.

Conclusion

1. The following does not address our fifth circle of application, the natural creation. For practical help in this realm, see the resources listed in chap. 11, nn. 1–2.

GENERAL INDEX

131–32; obligations of, 158–60;
suffering of, 187–90
church, the, 100, 133–35, 207n1;
mission of, 138; tasks of,
47–48; the world's view of, 138
communication, verbal and
nonverbal, 25, 45, 63, 73, 195;
nonverbal communication,
30–32; relationship between
verbal and nonverbal dimensions of communication,
29–30; verbal and nonverbal
witness, 127; verbal versus
nonverbal communication,
26–27. *See also* nonverbal communication, types of
consumerism, 147
creation, 98–99, 120, 147–48, 197;
redemption of, 115–16

DeYoung, Kevin, 151

emoticons, 28–29
Ephesians, book of, division of
into two halves, 79–80
evangelism, 49–50, 54–55. *See also*
evangelism, verbal aspects of
evangelism, verbal aspects of,
47–48; and eclipsing the verbal
witness, 48–50; and incarnation, 209n1 (chapter 6)

faith, 16, 19, 42, 195; and works,
80–82, 209n2
Francis of Assisi, 12
Franciscans, 12, 207n2
fundamentalists, 18–19

Gentiles, 96
God, 48, 91, 145, 157, 158, 166,
172, 200, 204, 205, 211n3;
affirmations of in the Bible,
151–52; image of, 112–14;
intent of for Israel, 155–56;

intention for his creation, 60;
invisible qualities of, 123–24,
207–8n5; judgment of, 145;
mercy of, 171; misunderstanding of God's methods, 55–59;
plan of for the world, 143–44,
146; power of for salvation, 54,
57–58; preference of for the
poor, 213–14n4; sovereignty of,
197; wisdom of, 55, 56; working of his salvation through
Christ crucified, 57–58. *See
also* God, covenant people of;
God, vice-regents of; kingdom
of God, the
God, covenant people of, 171
"God in the Dock" (Lewis),
122–23
God, vice-regents of, 142–44
Goethe, Johann, 111
gospel, the, 35–36, 45, 100, 147;
differences in Jesus's and
Paul's gospel messages, 40–41;
enacting of, 75, 131; power of,
52–53; proclaiming of, 75
gospel, the, and the mistaken
strategy that we can preach the
gospel without words, 41–42;
and the cognitive content of
the gospel, 42–43; misplacing
the power of the gospel, 50–55;
New Testament preaching and
teaching verbs, 44; and verbs
for preaching, 43–44
gospel versus the epistles, 152–54
gospel-worthy conduct, 83,
145–48; in family life, 85–86;
as God's people, 86–90; and
the natural creation, 98–99;
in personal life, 83–85; and
society at large, 90–98
gospel-worthy deeds, 131–35
Gospels, the, 153
Great Commandment, the, 51, 53

SCRIPTURE INDEX